A HISTORY OF THEATRICAL ART

A History of Theatrical Art

In Ancient and Modern Times by

Karl Mantzius

Authorised Translation by

Louise von Cossel

Volume III

The Shakespearean Period
in England

GLOUCESTER, MASS.

PETER SMITH

1970

First Published, 1904
Reprinted, 1937
Reprinted, 1970

CONTENTS

viii CONTENTS

LIST OF ILLUSTRATIONS

THE THEATRES

I

Before the Existence of Theatres—Influence of Italian stage technique
—Inns—Attacks of the Puritans—James Burbage and the Erection of
the First Theatre.

AT the date of Shakespeare's birth (1564) no permanent
theatre as yet existed in England.

But there had long existed a class of professional
actors, descended partly from the mystery and miracle
playing artisans of the Middle Ages, partly from the
strolling players, equilibrists, jugglers and jesters.[1]

Professional Italian actors (players of the *Commedia
dell'Arte*), who in the sixteenth century spread their gay
and varied art all over Europe, also supplied English
players with that touch of professional technique, in
which their somewhat vacillating and half amateurish
art was still wanting.

While, however, as far as France is concerned, the
Italian influence must strike everybody who studies the

---

[1] As early as the ninth year of the reign of Henry VII. we find in a
royal account-book the following among other entries : . . . *Item*, payed
for two plaies in the hall, 26s. 8d. *Item*, to the king's players for a reward,
100s. . . . *Item*, to the players that begged by the way, 6s. 8d. (quoted by
Malone : *Historical Account of the English Stage*, p. 43). Here we notice
already an interesting difference between the refined royal actors, who
receive 100s. in reward, as much as the king loses at cards, and the poor,
destitute jugglers who beg alms on the high-road of their passing
sovereign.

stage-history of the country, the evidence of a fertilisa-
tion of English scenic art by the *Commedia dell'Arte* is
scanty.   Yet I think it is sufficient to deserve more
attention than has hitherto been bestowed on it.

In any case there is sufficient evidence to prove that
Italian professional actors penetrated into England and
exercised their art there.

In January 1577 an Italian comedian came to London
with his company.   The English called him Drou-
siano, but his real name was Drusiano Martinelli, the
same who with his brother Tristano visited the court
of Philip II.; and there is no reason to suppose that he
was either the first or the last of his countrymen who
tried to carry off good English gold from merry London.
The typical Italian masks are quite well known to the
authors of that period.   Thus Thomas Heywood mentions all these Doctors, Zannis, Pantaloons and Harlequins,
in which the French, and still more the Italians, distinguished themselves.[1]   In Kyd's *Spanish Tragedy*, and
in Ben Jonson's *The Case is Altered*, mention is made
of the Italian improvised comedy, and a few well-known
types of character in the dramatic literature of the time
bear distinct traces of having been influenced by Italian
masks; *e.g.* Ralph Roister Doister in Udall's comedy of

[1] Thom. Heywood: *An Apology for Actors*, 1612; reprinted by the
Shakespeare Society, 1841, p. 43.   Comp. also the passage in Shakespeare's
As You Like It, ii. 7 :—
"The sixth age shifts
Into the lean and slipper'd pantaloon,
With spectacles on nose and pouch on side ;
His youthful hose, well saved, a world too wide
For his shrunk shank ; and his big manly voice,
Turning again toward childish treble, pipes
And whistles in his sound."

that name; as well as the splendid Captain Bobadill and his no less amusing companion, Captain Tucca, in Ben Jonson's *Every Man in his Humour* and *The Poetaster*, all of which are reproductions of the typical Capitano.

However, it is not these literary testimonies that I consider the most striking evidence of the influence of Italian professional technique on English professional actors. It is a remarkable discovery made by the highly esteemed Shakespearean archæologist, Edmond Malone, about a century ago, in Dulwich College, that mine of ancient English dramatic research, founded by the actor Edward Alleyn.

Among the notes left by the old pawnbroker and theatrical manager, Henslowe, and the various papers, letters, parts, accounts, etc., of his son-in-law, the famous and very wealthy actor Alleyn, among these rare documents, to which we owe a great part of our knowledge of the Shakespearean stage, Malone found four remarkable card-board tables, on which the plots of as many plays were put down, together with the names of the persons represented, their entrances and exits, cues for music, sennets, etc.

According to Collier's description,[1] these tables—one of which only is preserved, the three others having disappeared through the carelessness and disorder which at that time prevailed in the Dulwich treasury—were about fifteen inches in length and nine in breadth. They

[1] J. P. Collier: *English Dramatic Poetry*, iii. p. 197 (edit. 1879). In Malone's *Additions to the Historical Account*, we find four reprints of these tables, with explanations partly by Malone himself, partly by Steevens.

were divided into two columns, and between these, towards the top of the table, there was a square hole for hanging it up on a hook or some such thing.   They bore the following titles :—

1. The Plotte of the Deade Man's Fortune ;
2. The Plotte of the First Parte of Tamar Cam ;
3. The Plotte of Frederick and Basilea and
4. The Platte of the Secound Parte of the Seven Deadlie Sinns.

The last mentioned play is known for certain to have been composed by the excellent comic actor, Richard Tarlton.   Gabriel Harvey, the astrologist and the implacable antagonist of Thomas Nash, tells us in his letters [1] how Tarlton himself in Oxford invited him to see his celebrated play on *The Seven Deadly Sins* ; Harvey asked him which of the seven was his own deadly sin, and he instantly replied : " By G— the sinne of other gentlemen, lechery."

Tarlton died in the year 1588, and some of the other plays, especially *The Dead Man's Fortune*, are considered to be a good deal older than his.   They belong, therefore, to an early period of the English Renaissance stage.

These four tables caused considerable trouble to Malone and his contemporary Steevens, as well as to later investigators, as they are without equals in the archæology of the English stage.   If these men had known that such tables, containing the plot of the piece which was acted at the time, were always hung up on the stage of the Italian *Commedia dell'Arte* in order to

---

[1] [Gabriel Harvey :] Four letters and certain Sonnets, 1592, p. 29.

assist the memory of the improvising actors, they would have seen instantly that their essential historical importance to us consists in their showing by documentary evidence how the early Elizabethan scenic art in its outer form was influenced and improved by the Italians.

The fact that one of the principal characters in the oldest scenario (*The Dead Man's Fortune*) bears the name of *Panteloun* further confirms this supposition.

This is not the place to investigate how far the English were influenced by Italian professional dramatic art. At any rate, the English national character differed too much from the Italian to allow it to receive more than an outward and formal stamp. And even this superficial effect is much less significant in England than in France. Still we are certainly not mistaken in assuming that it helped to strengthen English dramatic art, which already possessed no small amount of power ; and we may take it for granted that about the time of Shakespeare's birth, London possessed a socially and professionally organised class of actors, in spite of the fact that they did not yet possess a theatre of their own.

Before proper theatres were built, and after the time of the great Mysteries, the actors found a refuge for their art chiefly in the Inns, those splendid and expensive old public-houses which convey to our minds the idea of old-fashioned and picturesque comfort; where the nobility and clergy sought their quarters in winter, and where the carriers unloaded their goods in the large square yards, which were surrounded on all sides by the walls of the inn. On these walls there were galleries running all round, supported by wooden pillars and with steep picturesque ladders leading up to them.

It was in these yards—of " The Cross Keys " in Gracechurch Street, of " The Bull " in Bishopsgate Street, " La Belle Sauvage " on Ludgate Hill, or the " Tabard Inn " in Southwark—that the actors set up their stages. Perhaps it was this very circumstance that became one of the indirect reasons why they were finally obliged to build a house for themselves.

Certainly the inns offered advantages to the actors ; they were meeting-places for the public, frequented by lords and other persons of distinction ; probably the companies paid next to nothing for the use of them. In themselves they afforded good room for the audience, with a natural pit for ordinary people in the yard, and with more comfortable " boxes " for the more distinguished part of the audience on the surrounding balconies and at the windows facing the yard.

On the other hand, these inn-theatres had their drawbacks. In the first place, the actors were not on their own ground, and so, after all, they were only tolerated. Secondly, it must have been very difficult for them to keep to regular prices, and especially to secure the payment of the entrance fee, as they had probably to collect the money during or after the performance, thus depending on the liberality of the public for their remuneration. And finally, worst of all, they were led into quarrels with the Lord Mayor and with the citizens.

Indeed, it is not unlikely that these performances in the inns caused a good deal of noise and disturbance in

1—An Old London Inn—Tabard Inn (from an 18th century illustration).

the quarters where they took place, and that the joyous, but by no means refined or quiet "pit," when going home, excited by one of Tarlton's jigs and by the strong ale of the inn, was not animated by very respectful feelings towards their sour Puritan fellow-citizens, who were scandalised as they watched "merry London" crowding past their windows. Nor is it improbable that these anything but respectful feelings vented themselves in some of the coarse expressions in which the plays of those times abound, where Puritanism, the sworn enemy, is concerned; "this barbarous sect," as it is called by a modern English author,[1] "from whose inherited and contagious tyranny this nation is as yet but imperfectly released."

It is certain, at any rate, that the Puritan citizens entertained a deep and sincere hatred of anything connected with plays and actors, and if it had been in their power to do what they liked, the world would once for all have been relieved of such pernicious and wicked vagabonds as William Shakespeare, Christopher Marlowe and Ben Jonson.

Fortunately, however, this power did not lie with the Puritans only.

Luckily, this sect, which like a malicious growth seemed to have gathered to itself all the stubbornness, insensibility and rude obstinacy of the nation, was counterbalanced by a refined and intellectual nobility, which was inspired by the new artistic and philosophical thought of the Renaissance, and seemed to foresee, if not fully to recognise, what a mine of poetry the English theatre of

---

[1] A. C. Swinburne : *A Study of Ben Jonson*, p. 43.

those times was destined to be. Thanks to men like Sir Francis Walsingham, Lords Leicester, Nottingham, Strange and Sussex, the drama resisted for a time the violent and unwearied attacks of the Puritans. Most fortunately for the actors also, Queen Elizabeth, as well as her successors, James I. and Charles I., was fond of plays, and favourably inclined towards their performers.

Elizabeth rendered a great service to the actors by placing them under the patronage of the nobility. The municipal authorities, who were frequently Puritan, considered neither dramatic art nor dramatic poetry as an acceptable means of livelihood ; consequently, those who cultivated these noble arts easily exposed themselves to being treated as " masterless men," unless they could give a reference to some distinguished aristocratic name.

The Queen ordered by law—in a statute which has often been misunderstood—" that all common players of interludes wandering abroad, other than players of interludes belonging to any baron of this realme, or any other honourable personage of greater degree, to be authorised to play under the hand and seale of arms of such baron or personage, shall be adjudged and deemed rogues and vagabonds " ; in other words, the Queen urged all actors, for their own sakes, to place themselves under the patronage of some nobleman, in order to protect them against the persecution of the Puritan citizens.

But even such mighty protection could not entirely shield them, and it was this very power of the London Corporation to injure the actors that caused the establishment of the first London theatre.

In the year 1572 the Plague broke out in London ;

it killed many thousands of people, and kept recurring at certain intervals during the next twenty or thirty years, carrying horror and death with it. Under these circumstances all dramatic performances were prohibited for a time in London, a precaution which was reasonable enough, as the dense crowding of people might have helped to spread the disease. But the magistrate seems to have caught eagerly at this opportunity of interfering.

In Harrison's " Description of England " the event is reported as follows : " Plaies are banished for a time out of London, lest the resort unto them should ingender a plague, or rather disperse it, being alredy begonne. Would to God these comon plaies were exiled for altogether as semenaries of impiety, and their theatres pulled downe as no better than houses of baudrie. It is an evident token of a wicked time when plaiers wesce so rich that they can build suche houses. As moche I wish also to our comon beare baitinges used on the sabaothe daies." [1]

We cannot help noticing the predilection of the Puritans for the coarse bear-fights, which in their opinion were only displeasing to God when performed on a Sabbath, whereas the play-houses at any time were no better than the "ill-famed stews" in Southwark. It cannot be denied, however, that, under the prevailing circumstances, it was quite right that the play-houses should be temporarily forbidden.

[1] Harrison's *Description of England*, edited by F. J. Furnivall, i. p. 54. From this report it might seem as if there existed permanent theatres as early as 1572, but Harrison's annals are continued down to 1592, and, as Ordish (*Early London Theatres*, p. 31) justly points out, he may have written this passage at any period between 1572 and 1592. Harrison has confused what happened in 1572 with his own reflections about later events.

But the sudden and unwarranted expulsion of all dramatic performances from the precincts of London a few years later (1575) cannot be accounted for otherwise than by the increasing popularity which these plays enjoyed among the non-Puritan public, and the envy with which the clergy saw the people crowding much more to the places where actors interpreted the rising poets, than to those where the preachers themselves enunciated their gloomy doctrine.

In the year 1574 the actor, James Burbage, father of the afterwards famous Richard Burbage, with four other actors, all belonging to the retinue of the Earl of Leicester, had received permission from the Queen to perform all kinds of plays anywhere in England, "for the recreation of her beloved subjects as well as for her own comfort and pleasure, if it should please her to see them."

Perhaps it was a countermove on the part of the Puritan community when the Lord Mayor and the Corporation in the following year straightway forbade all plays within the precincts of the town. If so, it proved a failure. James Burbage resolutely hired a liberty outside the city, and here, in 1576, on the premises of an ancient Roman Catholic priory, he built the first English play-house, which he named "The Theatre."

In the following year "The Theatre" gained an ally in "The Curtain," which was built in the same neighbourhood, both of course causing great indignation among the Puritans. In 1577, the year after the first play-house had been erected, there appeared a furious pamphlet (by John Northbrooke[1]) against "dicing, dancing, plays and interludes as well as other idle pastimes."

The treatise is written in the form of a dialogue, and the colloquists, Youth and Old Age, enter upon the subject in the following terms :—

Youth.—"Do you speake against those places also, whiche are made uppe and builded for such playes and enterludes as the Theatre and Curtaine is, and other such like places besides ?"

Age.—"Yea, truly ; for I am persuaded that Satan hath not a more speedie way and fitter schoole to work and teach his desire, to bring men and women into his snare of concupiscence and filthie lustes of wicked whoredome, than those places and plays and theatres are; and therefore necessary that those places and players shoulde be forbidden, and dissolved, and put downe by authoritie, as the brothell houses and stewes are."[2]

And no doubt all possible means were taken to have plays forbidden and the play-houses pulled down, but though the attack of the Black Army never ceased for a moment, the Puritans did not succeed in getting the better of the theatres till the year 1642, when they acquired political power through the Civil War ; and, fortunately for the part of mankind which appreciates

[1] Edited by T. P. Collier.

[2] The "Stews," houses of ill-fame, were mostly situated in Southwark. They were not prohibited by the authorities, and stood under the supervision of the Bishop of Winchester (Northbrooke's *Treatise against Dicing, Dancing, Plays and Interludes*, etc., edited by T. P. Collier).

art, this precious flower of culture, one of the richest and most remarkable periods in the life of dramatic art had developed into full bloom before the outbreak of the war.

Now and then in the course of this history we shall have opportunities of returning to the struggle between the theatres and the Puritans. At present we will only quote a further example of the attacks during the time of the earliest theatres, an example which not only shows the Puritan hatred of actors, which has been sufficiently indicated, but also the general favour with which the new theatrical enterprises were at once received.

In a sermon of 1578 we read the following bitter and deep-drawn sigh by the clergyman, John Stockwood: " Wyll not a fylthye playe wyth the blast of a trumpette sooner call thyther a thousande than an houres tolling of a bell bring to the sermon a hundred?—nay, even heere in the Citie, without it be at this place and some other certaine ordinarie audience, where shall you finde a reasonable company?—whereas, if you resort to the Theatre, the Curtayne and other places of playes in the Citie, you shall on the Lords Day have these places, with many other that I cannot recken, so full as possible they can throng." [1]

[1] Quoted by J. A. Halliwell-Phillipps : *Outlines of the Life of Shakespeare*, 3rd edition, p. 400.

II

"The Theatre" and its History—The Performances merely a Branch of
Sport—The Quarrel between Burbage and George Allen—The Staff
and Répertoire of "The Theatre"—The Second Theatre, "The
Curtain."

THAT the bold defiance with which James Burbage
and the other actors met the Lord Mayor and the
Corporation should prove so successful, lay almost in
the nature of things. The prohibition of plays within
the bounds of the city of London did not mean that
they were looked upon with animosity by the people,
but merely that a majority in the Corporation was
unfriendly to them. It was soon shown that, though
the wise city fathers could easily forbid the actors to
perform their plays in London, they could not prevent
the enthusiastic public from walking in crowds a mile
out of town in order to see such performances, especially
as people were quite accustomed to the journey.
Burbage, who was a business-like man, had chosen
his ground quite close to the public places, where the
Londoners practised their open air sports, and amused
themselves with tennis and football, stone-throwing,
cock-fights and archery.

Burbage gave his new building the name of "The
Theatre." The title was not intended to mean *the* theatre
par excellence, for the word theatre was not then commonly used to denote a building in which dramatic
representations were performed. It is more probable
that he thought he had succeeded in choosing an elegant

name with a certain suggestion of the old classics, which was euphonious and not quite common.

The usual name for a theatre was the play-house,[1] a house intended for all kinds of games and sport, such as fencing, bear-fights, bull-fights, jigs, morris-dances and pantomimes, as well as for dramatic performances.

It cannot be sufficiently emphasised that the theatrical entertainments of those times were something more or less literary, anyhow something quite apart from the dramatic performances of the present day. They were meant to satisfy mixed desires in the nation; but besides satisfying its craving for beautiful, picturesque language, fine spectacles and merry jests, they also gratified its desire for the display of physical strength, for shallow rhyming tricks and competitions, graceful exercises of the body, indeed for all that might be included under the notion of sport, and give opportunity for betting.

Therefore, the plays, properly so-called, alternated with fights between animals, in which bears and bulls were baited by great bloodthirsty bull-dogs, or with fencing matches fought by celebrated English and foreign fencing masters, with rope-dancing, acrobatic tricks and boxing. Even the serious performances ended with a more or less absurd jig, in which the clown sang endless songs about the events of the day, and danced interminable morris-dances.

Shakespeare and his contemporaries, whose works are now reckoned among the first literature—so much so that they are scarcely read any longer—at the time of which we are speaking were nothing but practical play-

---

[1] Play-house, from the Anglo-Saxon *plegahus; plega*=play, game, sport.

wrights, and Shakespeare was so far from dreaming that the time would come when his plays would be counted among the most precious treasures of posterity that, as we know, he did not even take the trouble to have a printed edition of his works published.

The many fighting scenes in the plays of the time, in Shakespeare's among the rest, the wrestling match in *As You Like It*, the duel between Macduff and Macbeth, the fencing scene between Hamlet and Laertes, no doubt afforded opportunities for magnificent displays of skill in the use of arms and in physical exercises, and we may be sure that the spectators followed those scenes with an interest which was perhaps more of a sporting than of a literary nature.

It was according to a well-calculated plan, therefore, that the elder Burbage erected his play-house north of the city in Finsbury Fields, where from ancient times the people had been accustomed to see and practise military exercises and other sports, and where the soldiers were still in the habit of practising archery and musketry.

And it was with equally sound calculation that he gave the theatre its particular form, which remained essentially the same in all the play-houses of the Shakespearean period.

Before the establishment of permanent theatres there had long existed amphitheatres for the performance of fights between animals, the so-called "Rings." These Rings—the auditorium as well as the arena—were open all round, and the seats, like those of the ancient Greek theatre, were placed according to the natural formation of the ground.

Burbage retained the circular amphitheatrical form. Being a joiner as well as an actor and manager, he was no doubt his own architect in his new theatrical enterprise.

But instead of the roofless, open air auditorium, he constructed a covered circular wooden building with storeys or galleries, which was made so as to contain a number of boxes for the distinguished and well-paying public, and which entirely enclosed the open uncovered arena, which, as it recalled the inn-yards, was called "the yard," or afterwards, perhaps on account of the high pit-like construction surrounding it, "the pit," whence the poorest and humblest spectators enjoyed the performances.

Finally, he built a covered "tire-house" or "tiring-house"—as it was called in those times—for the actors, a place in which also all the requisites and the so-called "properties" were kept. This tiring-house stood within the circle, and its roof towered up above the auditorium.

From the tiring-house the stage—a simple wooden platform resting on rams—was pushed forward, and it might be removed when the arena was to be used for fights between animals, etc., instead of dramatic performances.

By this reform of the building—a reform which became epoch-making to the whole Shakespearean period —James Burbage obtained a threefold advantage : more comfortable seats for the more distinguished portion of the audience, where they were sheltered from wind and weather ; the use of the house both for plays and the baiting of animals ; and the power to oblige the public to pay their admission at certain doors of his building, which spared him the unpleasant and unsafe collection of money from spectators, who might not always be very willing to pay.

But this result was not obtained without considerable expense.

Though we are not so fortunate as to possess a drawing of the outside or inside of " The Theatre," about the shape of which, therefore, we must partly draw our conclusions from analogy with other play-houses, we are comparatively well informed as to its outward history till it was pulled down in 1598-99.

Thus we know that the enterprise cost James Burbage £666, 13s. 4d., a considerable sum in those days, which would be equal to about eightfold that amount in our own time.

This money Burbage borrowed of his father-in-law, John Braynes, to whom he had to pay high interest, and it represented only the cost of the building itself, for he did not buy the ground on which it stood.   This ground belonged to one Giles Allen, and in the contract between him and Burbage it was settled, among other points, that if, in the course of the first ten years after the drawing up of the lease, Burbage spent a sum of £200 or more on the building, he should have a right to remove it after the expiration of the lease.

The lease was drawn up in the year 1576, for a period of twenty-one years.   In spite of many pecuniary difficulties which the heavy rent and high interest naturally entailed on Burbage—who for some time even seems to have been obliged to mortgage his entire property—and innumerable annoyances from the Puritans, Burbage succeeded in keeping his theatre above water till the expiration of the lease and till his own death, which occurred in 1597.

But before this date he had been negotiating with the proprietor, Giles Allen, about a prolongation of the lease. Allen, who was evidently as grasping as he was difficult to deal with, and who may not unjustly be suspected of having been an instrument in the hands of the Puritan authorities, had caused him a good deal of trouble in the course of years.   On seeing how people crowded to the theatre, he had tried, for one thing, to press Burbage for a higher rent, and, partly for religious, partly for moral reasons, had threatened to forbid the running of a play-house on his property.   The negotiations about the new lease had not come to an end when the elder Burbage died, and left his two sons, Cuthbert, who was a bookseller, and Richard, who was the leading actor of his time, not only burdened with the play-house, the long lease of which had expired, but opposed by a proprietor with whom it was impossible to come to terms, and by a magistrate who was more eager than ever to deal a blow at the play-houses.

In the same year, when the two brothers took on " The Theatre," the Lord Mayor of London actually succeeded in inducing the Privy Council to issue an order of suppression against it and other play-houses. The order begins as follows : " Her Majestie being informed that there are verie greate disorders committed in the common playhouses both by lewd matters that are handled on the stages, and by resorte and confluence of bad people, hathe given direction that not onlie no playes shall be used within London or about the Citty, or in any public place, during this tyme of sommer, but that also those playhouses that are erected and built only for suche purposes shall be plucked downe, namelie the Curtayne and the Theatre nere to Shorditch, or any other within that county." [1]

It is not known whether the order was withdrawn or whether the disregard of it was winked at—the court very likely was not particularly inclined to see the sentence of condemnation carried out — at all events, neither " The Curtain " nor " The Theatre " was pulled down at the time. But the order shows how much power the Puritan citizens possessed, and what difficulties the brothers Burbage had to contend with.

They seem, however, to have inherited their father's resolute character. Since it seemed quite impossible to come to terms with the grasping proprietor, Allen, the brothers were sensible enough to avail themselves of the clause in the now expired lease, which permitted them to pull down and remove the buildings they had erected on the premises, in case they had spent at least £200 on them during the first ten years.

This sum had been much exceeded at the time, and one day, to the great consternation and anger of the astonished Giles Allen, they simply removed " The Theatre."

One of the paragraphs in the account of the subsequent law-suit between Allen and the Burbages gives a very vivid idea of this remarkable removal. Allen accuses Cuthbert Burbage of " unlawfullye combininge and confederatinge himselfe with the sayd Richard

[1] Halliwell-Phillipps : *Outlines of the Life of Shakespeare*, 3rd ed., p. 403.

Burbage and one Peeter Streat, William Smyth and divers other persons, to the number of twelve, to your subject unknowne, did aboute the eight and twentyth daye of December in the one and fortyth yeere of your Highnes raygne [1598] . . . ryoutouslye assemble themselves together, and then and there armed themselves with dyvers and manye unlawfull and offensive weapons, as, namelye, swordes, daggers, billes, axes and such like, and so armed, did then repayre unto the sayd Theater, and then and there, armed as aforesayd, in verye ryotous, outragious and forcyble manner, and contrarye to the lawes of your highnes realme, attempted to pull downe the sayd Theater, whereuppon divers of your subjectes, servauntes and farmers, then goinge aboute in peaceable manner to procure them to desist from that their unlawfull enterpryse, they the sayd ryotous persons aforesayd notwithstanding procured then therein with greate vyolence, not only then and there forcyblye and ryotouslye resisting your subjectes, servauntes and farmers, but allso then and there pulling, breaking and throwing downe the sayd Theater in verye outragious, violent and riotous sort, to the great disturbance and terrefyeing not onlye of your subjectes sayd servauntes and farmers, but of divers others of your Majesties loving subjectes there neere inhabitinge ; and having so done, did then alsoe in most forcible and ryotous manner take and carrye away from thence all the wood and timber thereof unto the Bancksyde in the parishe of St Marye Overyes, and there erected a newe playehowse with the sayd timber and wood."

Such was the precipitate end of the first short-lived

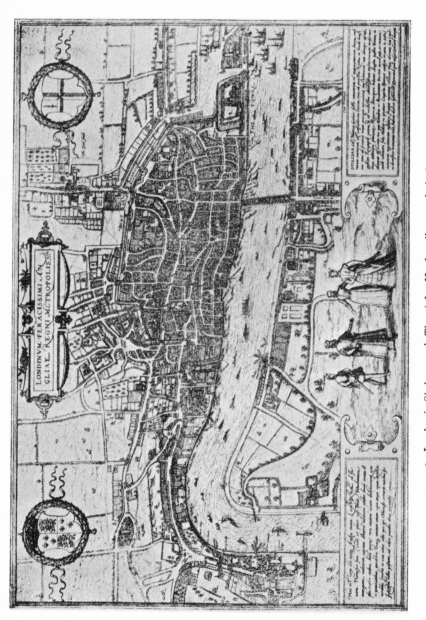

2—London in Shakespeare's Time (after Hoefnagel's ground-plan).

London play-house. But the new house, which was built out of its materials on the "Bankside," was the celebrated "Globe," the name of which is inseparably connected with that of Shakespeare.

As we said above, James Burbage, the creator of "The Theatre," belonged to the company which played under the patronage of Lord Leicester, and therefore went under the name of "Lord Leicester's Servants" or "Men." The four other actors, who in 1574 received a royal licence to act from Queen Elizabeth, were John Perkin, John Lanham, William Jonson, and Robert Wilson.

While James Burbage was no doubt the leader of the company, Robert Wilson is supposed to have been its chief actor, at all events of comic parts, and he was the only one among the five who was also a dramatic author. Under his name, but after his death, Cuthbert Burby[1] published in 1594 *The Prophecy of the Cobbler* ; and among anonymous plays the following are ascribed to him : *Fair Em, the Miller's Daughter from Manchester* ; *The Three Ladies of London,* etc.[2]

Most likely some of Wilson's plays were acted in "The Theatre." With this exception the internal history of this play-house is rather obscure, and very little is known of its répertoire. A few titles may be found in contemporary literature, such as *The Blacksmith's Daughter,* mentioned by the Puritan Gosson[3] in his

---

[1] A variant of Burbage. The Danish original does not contain this note, and I have not been able to find the variant "Burbay" anywhere but on this page.—L. v. C.

[2] Comp. F. G. Fleay : *A Biographical Chronicle of the English Drama,* under "Robert Wilson, senior," ii. pp. 278, ff.

[3] Gosson : *School of Abuse,* p. 30. *The Conspiracies of Catilina* is mentioned by Gosson as "a pig of my owne Sowe," as it was written by himself.

"School of Abuse," as " containing the treachery of Turks, the honourable bountye of a noble mind, the shining of vertue in distresse," "The Conspiracy of Catilina," "Cæsar and Pompey," and "The Play about the Fabians."

All these must have belonged to the earliest répertoire of " The Theatre," for Gosson's " School of Abuse " appeared in 1579.

It is of more interest that Thomas Lodge [1] mentions the original pre-Shakespearean *Hamlet* as having been acted in " The Theatre." He speaks of one who "looks as pale as the visard of the ghost which cries so miserably at the Theater, like an oister-wife, ' Hamlet, revenge.' "

The same company, originally " Lord Leicester's Servants," continued to act in " The Theatre " till it was pulled down. But the company several times changed its patron and consequently its name. In 1588 Lord Leicester died, and after his death Ferdinando Stanley, Lord Strange, became the patron of the company; till 1592, therefore, the actors were called " Lord Strange's Men." But in 1592 Lord Strange was created Earl of Derby; consequently the troupe became for two years " The Earl of Derby's Men." In 1594 the Earl of Derby died, and Henry Carey, first Lord Hunsdon and Lord Chamberlain, undertook to become patron of the company, which, therefore, adopted the name of " The Lord Chamberlain's Servants." The son of Lord Hunsdon, George Carey, second Lord Hunsdon, after his father's death in 1596, also inherited the patronage of the actors, and for almost a year they had to content themselves with being called " Lord Hunsdon's Men,"

---

[1] Th. Lodge : *Wit's Miserie*, 1596.

until Lord Hunsdon became Lord Chamberlain like his father, and allowed the company to resume the title of " The Lord Chamberlain's Servants " (1597). This name the actors retained till the accession of King James in 1603, after which they were promoted to the title of " The King's Players"; this title put them in the first rank, which indeed they had long held in reality, and which they kept till the suppression of the play-houses in 1642.

It is no slight task for one who desires to study theatrical affairs in the time of Shakespeare to make himself acquainted with the varying names of the companies of actors ; but without such knowledge it would be very difficult to pursue the thread of the history even of the leading companies.

About the year 1590 our company received an addition in the person of a young man, who was not only a skilled and useful actor, but who also possessed the accomplishment of being able to adapt older plays to the taste of the times, and even proved to have the gift of writing tolerably good plays himself, though older and jealous colleagues might hint at their not being altogether original. This young man, whose capacities became of no slight use to the company and " The Theatre," was named William Shakespeare.[1]

At this time the leading actors of " The Theatre " were the great tragedian Richard Burbage, who was then quite a young man, Henry Condell and John Heminge, who continued to be the mainstays of the company. There was also the clown, Augustine Phillips, an excellent

---

[1] It is impossible to give the exact date of Shakespeare's engagement at Burbage's theatre.

comic actor of the old school. These four became the most intimate friends of Shakespeare, and to Condell and Heminge posterity owes special gratitude, since it was they who, after the death of Shakespeare, undertook the publication of the first printed collection of his plays.

It is impossible to decide definitely which of Shakespeare's plays belonged to the répertoire of "The Theatre." It is probable that his first plays, *Love's Labour Lost*, *The Comedy of Errors*, *The Two Gentlemen of Verona*, and his first tragedy, *Romeo and Juliet*, saw the light on this stage between 1589 and 1591.[1] Afterwards, between 1594 and 1597, these were possibly increased by *A Midsummer Night's Dream*, *Richard the Second*, *King John*, *The Merchant of Venice* and *Henry IV*.

The répertoire of "The Theatre" also included the so-called "jigs," merry after-plays, mostly consisting of songs and dances, with frequent allusions to the events of the day, sneering at the Puritans, the magistrates and other enemies of the play-houses. Later, we shall have an opportunity of entering more closely into the character of the "jig."

It has been briefly mentioned above that not long after the establishment of "The Theatre"—at the latest in the following year—this play-house gained a companion in "The Curtain," which thus became the second of its kind in London.

The two play-houses were very close to each other, but for this very reason it seems natural to suppose

[1] Fleay : *The English Drama*, ii. p. 176, and *Life of Shakespeare.* Others are of the opinion that no drama of Shakespeare's appeared before 1591.   Comp. Sidney Lee : *Life of William Shakespeare*, p. 48.

that they were rather meant to support than to rival each other. They were like a kind of double-barrelled gun directed against the Corporation,[1] and they seem indeed, to an equal extent, to have roused the anger of the Puritans, for they are generally mentioned together in the Puritan pamphlets directed against play-houses and all other wickedness.

However, the history of "The Curtain" is almost unknown to us. While we know a good deal about the outward circumstances of "The Theatre" on account of the constant troubles which the Burbage family had to endure from the proprietor of the ground and the municipal authorities, and of the subsequent lawsuit, the reports we find about "The Curtain" are extremely meagre. We know neither when [2] nor by whom it was built, nor when it was pulled down.

By a mistake which is natural enough, its name has been connected with the front curtain of the stage. We shall see later that no such curtain existed in the time of Shakespeare, and we do not know that the background draperies of that period had the fixed name of "curtain."

Anyhow, the possibility of this derivation is absolutely excluded by the fact that the spot on which the second London play-house was built, for some unknown reason bore the name of "Curtayne Close."[3] So the play-house was simply named after the spot on which it was built.

---

[1] Ordish : *Early London Theatres*, p. 80.

[2] It was probably in 1577, for it is mentioned, together with "The Theatre," shortly after the erection of this building. However, it may have been built in the same year as the latter (1576), only a little later.

[3] Halliwell-Phillipps : *Outlines of the Life of Shakespeare*, 3rd ed., p. 422.

As long as "The Theatre" stood close beside it, the two companions shared almost the same fate. We have seen that in 1597 an order was issued to pull down both play-houses ; this order, however, was never carried out. But after the removal of "The Theatre" to Bankside, "The Curtain" seems to have gone its own way. The actors, on the whole, were not afraid of pleading their cause from the stage, and of retorting on the attacks of their assailants by lashing them with the whip of caricature, and it seems that those of "The Curtain" had gone a little too far in their Aristophanic parodies of their worthy fellow-citizens and chief magistrate. For in May 1601 the justices of the peace for the county of Middlesex received the following admonition from the Privy Council : "We doo understand that certaine players that use to recyte their playes at the Curtaine in Moorefeilds, do represent upon the stage in their interludes the persons of some gent of good desert and quality that are yet alive under obscure manner, but yet in such sorte as all the hearers may take notice both of the matter and the persons that are meant thereby. This beinge a thinge very unfitte, offensive and contrary to such direction as have been heretofore taken, that no plaies should be openly shewed but such as were first perused and allowed, and that minister no occasion of offence or scandall, wee do hereby require you that you do forthwith forbidd those players to whomsoever they appertaine that do play at the Courtaine in Moorefeildes to represent any such play, and that you will examine them who made that play and to shew the same unto you, and as you in your discrecions shall thincke the same unfitte to be publiquely shewed to forbidd them from henceforth to play the same eyther privately or publiquely ; and yf upon veiwe of the said play you shall finde the subject so odious and inconvenient as is informed, wee require you to take bond of the cheifest of them to aunswere their rashe and indiscreete dealing before us."

We know nothing of the result of this prosecution, but we may be allowed to assume that it did not result in very severe measures. We seem to read a certain concealed sympathy in the writ of the great Lords, and we cannot help suspecting that it was the Puritan citizens who felt themselves hit, and who brought the complaint. If the Lords had been the butt of the mockery, no doubt the proceeding of the actors would have appeared to them much worse than " rashe and indiscreete."

Until the Globe Theatre was built, the Burbages most likely possessed a share in " The Curtain." At any rate, their company used that building alternately with their own; no doubt, for instance, during the period between the pulling down of " The Theatre " and the building of " The Globe." During this period they played (as the "Lord Chamberlain's Men")[1] among other things no less famous a piece than Ben Jonson's *Every Man in his Humour*, which, according to old tradition, was accepted on the recommendation of Shakespeare, after having been put aside contemptuously by the other lead-

---

[1] The original editions of the plays of this time generally have after their title a note stating by what company they were acted (" ——, as acted by ——'s men "). Thus a knowledge of the varying names of the companies provides us with a pretty safe means of determining the date of the appearance of the plays.

ing actors. This splendid play had an enormous success.
Of Shakespeare's plays *Much Ado about Nothing* and
The Second Part of King Henry IV. were acted.

There is scarcely any reason for assuming with
Halliwell-Phillipps and Ordish, that the first performance
of *Henry V.* took place at "The Curtain." At the
appearance of this play (in 1599) the Globe Theatre
was built, and we cannot doubt that it was here that
this popular play saw the light. So the frequently
mentioned "wooden O" in the prologue does not allude
to "The Curtain," but to "The Globe."

The outward shape of "The Curtain" we must imagine
to have been, like that of "The Theatre," circular, and
unroofed in the centre. It is generally supposed to
have been somewhat smaller than Burbage's first theatre.

The last period of the existence of "The Curtain"
is enveloped in obscurity. But there is no reason to
suppose that it did not continue to exist till all play-
houses were put down during the Civil War, 1642-47.
If "The Curtain" was preserved as long as that, its life
was longer than that of any other play-house of the
Shakespearean period.

Interior of a Private Theatre
(Title to William Alabaster's *Roxana*).

III

The Blackfriars' Theatre—Its Comparatively Slight Importance to Shakespeare—Its Situation and Construction—Private and Public Theatres—The Question of Property—Children's Plays.

BEFORE his death the energetic James Burbage started another theatrical enterprise, the Blackfriars' Theatre.

In the reading world the name of the Blackfriars' Theatre has for a long time been connected almost as closely as that of "The Globe" with the dramatic and the histrionic work of Shakespeare, but this is correct only to a certain extent. It is true that Shakespeare appeared as an actor on this stage, and that some of his pieces were performed there, but his work at this theatre was only of very short duration, and the most important and glorious part of his career belongs exclusively to "The Globe," which, moreover, was the only theatre in which he had a pecuniary share as part-proprietor.

Until a few years ago the descriptions of the theatrical circumstances of the time by Shakespeare's biographers were chiefly based on the treatment of this subject by Malone and Collier, as given in the former's "Historical Account of the English Stage," and the latter's "Annals of the Stage."

Malone, who was unique in his time as an expert in theatrical archæology, brought forward an immense quantity of material to throw light on the theatrical circumstances of the time, and his honesty is above suspicion. However, as he himself confesses, he did not succeed in gaining a correct knowledge of the chronological details of the theatres themselves; and their history, on the whole, was not clear to him.

Of the honesty of Collier, the less said the better. His account of the history of the ancient theatres is a model of inaccuracy, even in the last edition of his large work, which appeared as late as 1879; besides which, his quite erroneous dates are put forth with the authoritative assurance which his once great name had given him. No wonder, therefore, that many later literary critics of Shakespeare have been tempted to adopt his entirely misleading chronology.

The last twenty or thirty years, however, have thrown abundant light on this question by the discovery of documents, which remove all doubt as to the outlines of the history of the most important theatres, though, so far as I know, no connected account of their external and internal history has yet been forthcoming.[1]

The present attempt to place the various theatres of the Shakespearean era in their correct relation to each other is essentially based on such documents as deeds of purchase, building-agreements, law-reports, petitions, etc.

On the 4th of February 1596 James Burbage bought a property which stood on ground belonging to the monastery of the Blackfriars, which is now pulled down, the " Blackfriars' precinct," as it was called. The site is now occupied by the imposing offices of " The Times," in

---

[1] T. F. Ordish, an expert in the topography of ancient London, has begun such a history, and begun it admirably. Unfortunately, he has not continued the work. The first part was published in 1894, and treats of the history of some of the theatres lying outside the town. The chapter by H. Barton Baker on the Elizabethan Theatres, in his *London Stage*, is too condensed and too inaccurate to be taken into serious consideration.

Queen Victoria Street near Blackfriars' Station.   In the days of Queen Elizabeth the open spaces in the Blackfriars' quarter were in great favour as tennis-courts. During the preceding reigns tennis had been forbidden in the Convent grounds, but Elizabeth willingly permitted respectable citizens, as well as strangers, foreign ambassadors and other noblemen, to practise on this spot the elegant game, which was as fashionable then as it is now.   But vagabonds, with apprentices and servants, who played against the will of their masters, were forbidden the use of this ground.[1]

When James Burbage chose this ground for the construction of a new theatre, he well knew what he was about, and he acted on the same practical principles which had guided him in selecting the site for " The Theatre."   It had previously been a pleasure-ground, not for the lower classes, but for noblemen and wealthy merchants, and it was a monastic ground with old "liberties," over which the chief magistrates of London had no control.

The old monastery had been partly rebuilt, and private suites of rooms had been arranged in it.   One of these private suites belonged to Sir Thomas More, and on the second floor there had formerly been a very large hall, which at the time we are writing of had been converted into seven spacious rooms, and lately inhabited by a physician, William de Lawne.   This property was bought by the elder Burbage for £600.[2]   What he

[1] Two royal licences for playing tennis in the Blackfriars' quarter have been found by Mr J. Greenstreet and published in *The Athenæum*, January 7th, 1888.

[2] The deed of purchase has been published by J. O. Halliwell-Phillipps in his *Outlines*, pp. 511-522.

meant to do was to restore the old hall to its original shape, and then to make a theatre of it.

Burbage probably began converting the private house into a theatre very soon after the purchase, for as early as November in the same year thirty-one inhabitants of the Puritan persuasion, among others, William de Lawne, the former owner of the building, brought a complaint before the Privy Council to prevent the change from taking place.

It is said in this complaint,[1] which is very characteristic : ". . . that whereas one Burbage hath lately bought certaine rooms in the same precinct neere adjoining unto the dwelling houses of the right honorable the Lord Chamberlaine and the Lord of Hunsdon, which romes the said Burbage is now altering, and meaneth very shortly to convert and turne the same into a comon playhouse, which will grow to be a very great annoyance and trouble, not only to all the noblemen and gentlemen thereabout inhabiting, but allso a generall inconvenience to all the inhabitants of the same precinct, both by reason of the great resort and gathering togeather of all manner of vagrant and lewde persons that, under cullor of resorting to the playes, will come thither and worke all manner of mischiefe, and also to the greate pestring and filling up of the same precinct, yf it should please God to send any visitation of sicknesse as heretofore hath been ; for that the same precinct is allready grown very populous, and besides that the same play-house is so neere the church that the noyse of the drummes and trumpetts will greatly dis-

[1] Halliwell-Phillipps, *Outlines*, 3rd edition, pp. 522, 523.

turbe and hinder both the ministers and parishioners in tyme of devine service and sermons, in tender consideracion whereof, as allso for that there hath not at any tyme heretofore been used any comon playhouse within the same precinct, but that now all players being banished by the Lord Mayor from playing within the Cittie by reason of the great inconveniences and ill rule that followeth them, they now thincke to plant themselves in liberties ; that therefore it would please your honors to take order that the same roomes may be converted to some other use, and that no playhouse may be used or kept there ; and your suppliants as most bounden shall and will dayly pray for your Lordships in all honor and happines long to live. . . ."

Of this petition the Privy Council seems not to have taken the slightest notice.   But it was the cause of a series of forgeries concocted and published by J. P. Collier, which represent petitions by various actors of Burbage's company, Shakespeare among the number, expressing a desire that the Blackfriars' Theatre may not be prohibited.   They also mention Shakespeare's share in it as being worth £933, 6s. 8d.   Collier tried to prove that the Blackfriars' Theatre was already built in 1576, and that Burbage and his company acted in it for a long time, and it was in support of these assertions that he produced his forgeries.   For the same purpose a letter was composed purporting to be from the Earl of Southampton to Sir Thomas Egerton, in which the Earl desires protection for the actors, mentioning Burbage and Shakespeare by name.   However, as late as 1596 the Blackfriars' Theatre was not yet ready for use, and it was not till many years later that Shakespeare and his company came to act in it.

Probably in the beginning of 1597 James Burbage finished his new play-house. It differed very much from the others ; indeed, it was only a large hall which was made into a stage and an auditorium. The hall, as we have seen, was on the second floor, and several winding flights of stone stairs led up to it. In contrast to " The Theatre " and " The Curtain," the whole space was covered—the leaden roof of the house is mentioned several times in the above-quoted deed of purchase. Later, these play-halls, which were arranged inside ordinary private houses, were called " private play-houses," as distinct from the larger open-air stages out of town, which were called " public play-houses."

Whether there existed any real difference between the private and the public play-houses, besides the fact that the former were smaller in size and under cover, has never been ascertained.

It may be supposed, however, that at the outset Burbage meant to collect a small and select aristocratic public in his new locality, and to exclude the tumultuous elements, which frequently caused annoyance to the actors in the pits of the public theatres ; and that for this reason he called his play-house " private," just as in English public-houses there is a " private room " for the more distinguished visitors, while the crowd must be contented with the " public room." It may be, indeed, that during its earliest years " The Blackfriars " had a more exclusive character, but later there appear distinct complaints that the owner has converted his theatre into a " publique playhowse, into which there is daily so great resort of people, and soe great multitude of coaches, whereof many are hackney-coaches bringing people of all sortes that sometimes all their streetes cannot conteyne them, that they endanger one the other, breake downe stalles, throw downe men's goodes from their shopps, hinder the passage of the inhabitantes there to and from their howses, lett the bringing in of their necessary provisions, that the tradesmen and shopp-keepers cannot utter their wares, nor the passengers go to the common water staires without danger of their lives and lyms, whereby manye times quarrells and effusion of blood hath followed, and the minister and people disturbed at the administration of the Sacrament of Baptisme and publique prayers in the afternoones. . . ."[1]

The enumeration of all these horrors, which, as we scarcely need observe, hails from the Puritan camp, shows what popularity this little theatre enjoyed after the death of Shakespeare, but it does not give us any clearer an idea than before of the difference between private and public theatres.

We must mention one more characteristic feature, which resulted from the establishment of a private theatre inside a house ; the effect, that is, that could be produced by playing sometimes in artificial light and sometimes in darkness by closing the shutters over the windows. From this effect the open air theatre was excluded. A contemporary author[2] says : " All the

[1] This quotation is taken from an order issued by the Corporation of London, who in 1619 wished to suppress " The Blackfriars." The order is quoted entire in Halliwell-Phillipps : *Outlines*, 3rd edition, p. 538.

[2] Thomas Dekker : *The Seven Deadly Sins of London*, etc., 1606 ; quoted by Malone, *Historical Account of the English Stage*, p. 63, n. 7.

city looked like a *private play-house*, when the *windows are clapt downe*, as if some *nocturnal* and dismal tragedy were presently to be acted."

The closed play-houses were probably lighted, in England as elsewhere, by chandeliers hung above the stage, to which a row of oil-lamps with double wicks seem to have been added later. Anyhow, this method of lighting is shown in an illustration (much more recent, it is true) of another private theatre " The Red Bull " (fig. 7). Compared with fig. 3, which may quite well represent " The Blackfriars," though we do not know for certain that it does, this drawing clearly shows that the scenic arrangements in the closed halls were essentially similar to those of the public play-houses.

It is quite possible that old James Burbage meant to fall back on Blackfriars, if he did not succeed in coming to terms with Giles Allen. However, he died, as we know, in 1597, the very year in which his play-house was arranged. This hall, therefore, was never used by the Burbage company, but was let to the well-known company called " The Children of the Chapel," or afterwards, " The Children of His Majesty's Revels," a company which enjoyed great favour at court in those times, and thus had particular reason to expect a large audience in the aristocratic quarter of Blackfriars.

In 1635 the bookseller Cuthbert Burbage writes the following lines about this matter to Lord Pembroke[1]

[1] On account of a complaint from some of " the King's players," who considered themselves prejudiced by C. Burbage, by this time the only surviving heir of his father James and his brother Richard. The various documents concerning this affair have been published by Halliwell-Phillipps (*Outlines*, pp. 539-551), and offer a most valuable contribution to our knowledge of the scenic conditions of the time.

(p. 549): . . . " The father of us, Cuthbert and Richard Burbage, was the first builder of playhowses, and was himselfe in his younger yeeres a player. 'The Theater' hee built with many hundred poundes taken up at interest. . . . Now for the Blackfriars, that is our inheritance; our father purchased it at extreame rates, and made it into a playhouse with great charge and troble; which after was leased out to one Evans that first sett up the boyes commonly called the Queenes Majesties Children of the Chappell. In processe of time, the boyes growing up to bee men, which were Underwood, Field, Ostler, and were taken to strengthen the King's service; and the more to strengthen the service, the boyes dayly wearing out, it was considered that house would bee as fitt for ourselves, and soe purchased the lease remaining from Evans with our money, and placed men players, which were Heminge, Condell, Shakespeare, etc., and Richard Burbage, who, for thirty-five yeeres paines, cost and labour, made meanes to leave his wife and children some estate, and out of whose estate soe many other players and their families have been mayntained."

That this statement of C. Burbage about Blackfriars is correct has been confirmed quite recently by a series of records [1] concerning the lease of the theatre, which give us also the date, hitherto unknown, at which " The King's Company " itself began acting at Blackfriars.

Henry Evans of Blackfriars, London, gentleman, hired the large " Hall," as the play-hall is called in the

---

[1] They are published in full by James Greenstreet in *The Athenæum*, 7th and 21st of April 1888.

proceedings, with the adjoining room of Richard Burbage, for twenty-one years at a rent of £70 a year.[1]

During the first few years, while the boy-actors were still all the fashion, Henry Evans no doubt did good business with his children-plays.   Everybody knows Shakespeare's complaint of "little eyasses that cry out," a passage to which we shall have an opportunity of returning later.

But after some years taste changed, the cleverest boys, like Nathaniel Field and the above-mentioned Underwood and Ostler, grew up, and it was difficult for Evans to find new actors; so difficult, indeed, that he had recourse to the expedient of tempting "gentlemen's children against their will and employing them as actors," for which " disorderly conduct and proceeding" he was sentenced by the Star Chamber.

Under these circumstances Evans grew tired of managing the theatre, which no longer brought him the income which he had expected, and in 1608[2] he prevailed on Richard Burbage to cancel the lease of twenty-one years.   Thereupon " The King's Players" came to occupy "the larger Hall."   And, as the record of the proceedings tells us, here they succeeded in gaining so much favour with the public that in one

[1] The lease for the twenty-one years was not signed till the year 1600, but it is distinctly mentioned in the proceedings that the hall was constantly (that is ever since its reconstruction) used for acting.   Did not Evans have it during the three intervening years (1597-1600)?   Did the children act under another manager?   Or did another grown-up company act previously at Blackfriars?   To these questions I have not succeeded in finding an answer.

[2] This appears from the record of the proceedings, dating from 1612, in which it is stated that during the last four years Burbage and his companions had received the proceeds of " The Blackfriars."

winter they took £1000 more than they were accustomed to get on the Bankside (that is, in "The Globe" Theatre).

Special mention is made of John Hemminge, a highly esteemed actor of "The King's Company," as one of the partners, but not of Shakespeare. Of course it is not impossible that the latter may have owned a share in the theatre, but there is nothing to prove it.

After the death of Richard Burbage, which occurred in 1619, "The Blackfriars" remained in the possession of the family, and "The King's Company" continued to act there as well as at "The Globe." There were eight shares in the small theatre in the City, while the larger "Globe" was divided into sixteen shares. In the year 1635 we find the eight shares thus divided: the comic actor, John Shancke, has two; Cuthbert Burbage, one; the tragic actor, Richard Robinson, one; the tragic actor, Joseph Taylor, one; John Lowin, an actor of distinction, one; the widow of Henry Condell, one; and the widow of John Underwood, one.

After that time there is no information about "The Blackfriars." No doubt it continued to exist till the Civil War, 1642; possibly it was used for acting up to 1647, when plays definitely stopped. But after the Restoration, in 1660, it was no longer used as a theatre, and very likely it was pulled down by the Puritans in the meantime.

As we have seen, the first period of its existence— from 1597-1608 — was occupied by the acting of the "Children of the Chapel."

The child-actors were mostly recruited from the

boy-choristers in the Chapel Royal.   They were trained
and instructed by older actors, and they seem to have
cultivated a caricaturing imitation of the real and celebrated actors,[1] a speciality by which they evidently succeeded for a time in attracting a large part of the public.

From the allusions in *Hamlet* it seems that the
actors at "The Globe" suffered great pecuniary loss on
account of these boy-actors, and even that they were
obliged to go touring in order to make their living.
It is in the second scene of the second act, in the
conversation between Hamlet and Rosencrantz about
the actors who are expected at Elsinore, that Shakespeare finds an opportunity of venting his annoyance at
these troublesome little rivals.   He begins thus :—

Hamlet. What players are they ?

Rosencrantz. Even those you were wont to take
delight in, the tragedians of the city.

Ham. How chances it they travel ? their residence,
both in reputation and profit, was better
both ways.

Ros. I think their inhibition comes by the means of
the late innovation.

Ham. Do they hold the same estimation they did
when I was in the city ? are they so
followed ?

Ros. No, indeed are they not.

Ham. How comes it ? do they grow rusty ?

Ros. Nay, their endeavour keeps in the wonted
pace ; but there is, sir, an aery of children,

---

[1] Comp. for instance Ben Jonson's *Poetaster*, which was written for and
performed by these boys.

little eyasses, that cry out on the top of question, and are most tyrannically clapped for't ; these are now the fashion. . . .

During this period " The Blackfriars" and its eyasses provided a particularly powerful attraction by serving Ben Jonson as a medium in an exceedingly sharp, literary and personal quarrel which he had to settle with some of his contemporary actors and authors. The principal sufferers were John Marston and Thomas Dekker, and the quarrel included some of the Henslowe-Alleyn actors ("The Lord-Admiral's Men"), who at this time mostly acted in "The Fortune" Theatre.

Ben Jonson afterwards maintained, in his well-known conversations with William Drummond, that the origin of this not very creditable theatrical quarrel lay with Marston. "He had," writes Drummond, "many quarrels with Marston, beat him, and took his pistol from him, wrote his *Poetaster* on him ; the beginning of them were that Marston represented him in the stage." [1]

If Marston began the quarrel — which is possible, though there is no evidence to prove that he had maliciously represented Jonson on the stage [2]—Jonson

[1] *Ben Jonson's Conversations with William Drummond*, edited by David Laing, London, 1892. In the above quotation a correction of the punctuation has been made by J. H. Penniman (*The War of the Theatres*), which gives a very different sense to the much debated passage. The original runs as follows : " . . . Marston represented him in the stage, in his youth given to venerie. He thought the use of a maide nothing in comparison to the wantonness of a wyfe. . . . " Mr Penniman puts a full stop after "the stage," and makes the words "in his youth . . . " begin a new period, thus : " . . . Marston represented him in the stage. In his youth given to venerie, he thought the use of a maide nothing in comparison . . . " The correction appears very plausible.

[2] F. G. Fleay thinks that Chrysoganus in *Histriomastix* by Marston is meant to represent Jonson, but he informs us at the same time that this

laid on far the more heavily when it came to his turn to
defend himself.   In *Every Man out of His Humour*, in
Cynthia's Revels, and especially in *The Poetaster*, he
completely turned the tables on Marston and his other
antagonists.   He had the two last acted by the Chapel-
boys, and they drew dense crowds of people to the
Blackfriars' Theatre, and afforded great amusement to
the public, to whom literary quarrels have always been a
favourite entertainment.

Quite apart from the wonderful Pantilius Tucca, who
probably is not a portrait, but, like his dramatic
kinsman, Captain Bobadill, an imitation of the typical
Italian Capitano, *The Poetaster* exhibits a unique gallery
of Jonson's friends and enemies, and though the events
of the play are supposed to take place in the time of the
Emperor Augustus in Rome, it gives a better idea of
contemporary literary life in London than many histories
of literature.

Under the mask of Horace, Jonson — with no
inopportune modesty — represents himself, and gives
himself the pleasure of punishing the dull and tedious
Crispinus, that is, Marston, by administering an emetic
to him, which makes him vomit all the crude and stilted
phrases with which he has encumbered his works.

But besides this principal attack he deals several
side-blows at his contemporaries among fellow-authors
and actors.   Dekker is very hard hit as Demetrius, and
with the actors of " The Fortune " Theatre Jonson

character is described as very sympathetic (*Chronicle of the English
Drama*, ii. 71).   I have had no access to Marston's *Histriomastix*—it is not
included in Bullen's edition of his works—so I am unable to express any
personal opinion about the resemblance of the portrait.

seems at the time to have lived in the most strained relations, but it is impossible to say, in every case, against whom the malicious sarcasms, which are showered down on the heads of his former companions, are directed.[1] No attack on Shakespeare is to be found in the play; it has even been suggested that the refined and noble Virgil was meant to represent him.

In spite of this Shakespeare retorted on behalf of his fellows. *The Poetaster* was brought out in 1601, and in an anonymous University play of the same year, *The Return from Parnassus*, the literary quarrel is mentioned. In a conversation between Richard Burbage and William Kemp, the latter says : " Few of the University men play well; they smell too much of that writer Ovid and that writer Metamorphosis, and talke too much of Proserpina and Juppiter. Why, here's our fellow Shakespeare puts them all downe, I, and Ben Jonson too. O that Ben Jonson is a pestilent fellow ! he brought up Horace giving the gods a pill, but our fellow Shakespeare hath given him a purge that made him berag his credit."

Upon which Burbage answers : " It's a shrewd fellow, indeed."

There has been much debate about the purge which Shakespeare is said to have given Jonson. It is clear enough that Shakespeare took up arms against Jonson's attacks on the actors, the attacks which were performed

[1] I suppose Æsop to be the celebrated tragedian Edward Alleyn, who is also called " Seven-and-a-half-share." More about this in a future chapter. Possibly Frisker is William Kemp.

by the boys.   In *Hamlet* his protest against this mode
of fighting appears indeed in a very direct form.   He
says of the youthful actors who, as is clear from *The
Poetaster*, were accustomed to parody their adult fellow-
players : " . . . and so berattle the common stages—so
they call them—that many wearing rapiers are afraid of
goose-quills and dare scarce come thither."

And the dialogue continues as follows :—

Hamlet. What, are they children ? who maintains
'em ? how are they escoted ? Will they pursue the
quality no longer than they can sing ? will they not say
afterwards, if they should grow themselves to common
players—as it is most like, if their means are no better
—their writers do them wrong to make them exclaim
against their own succession.

Ros. 'Faith, there has been much to do on both
sides ; and the nation holds it no sin to tarre them to
controversy ; there was for a while no money bid for
argument, unless the poet and the player went to cuffs
in the question.

The meaning of these words is as clear as possible
and needs no comment.   However, there is no "purge"
here which might cast a slur on the reputation of Jonson.
It has been supposed that Shakespeare's real rejoinder
to Jonson was to be found in *Troilus and Cressida*,[1]
where Ajax was meant to represent Jonson.   But,
though this is by no means an absurd suggestion in itself,
it seems improbable that this play was written until long
after the quarrel had been settled.

---

[1] F. G. Fleay : *A Biographical Chronicle of the English Drama*, ii.
p. 189, f.

On the other hand, it is not impossible, though it has not come to our knowledge, that there may be found in *Hamlet* or elsewhere a stronger and more direct rejoinder to Jonson. We only know the scene quoted above from the folio edition,[1] and it is quite natural that in this edition, which was introduced to the reading world by Jonson himself, any passages that might be personally offensive to him were left out. To judge from the quotation from *The Return from Parnassus* there seems not to be the slightest doubt that, somehow or other, Shakespeare took part in the quarrel. And that the company to which he belonged sided against Jonson, appears distinctly from the fact that they acted a strongly polemical play written by Dekker and Marston against Jonson. The title of it was *Satiromastix*, or, as it was also called, *The Untrussing of the Humorous Poet*— that is Jonson.

However this may be, through these quarrels the little stage of " The Blackfriars " gained a sudden and sensational notoriety, and its young actors won a transient fame, as well as probably a basis of artistic skill, which carried some of them safely through the dangerous turning-point in their lives, when the beards began to appear on their chins.

From Jonson's works we know the names of some of the Chapel-boys. He mentions Nathaniel Field, Salathiel Pavy, Thomas Day, John Underwood, Robert Baxter, John Frost, William Ostler, and Thomas Marston.

Of these Nathaniel Field was, and continued to be,

---

[1] It is not found in the two quarto editions of *Hamlet*.

by far the most celebrated. He also became a popular playwright. But several of the other boys likewise became actors of note.

IV

The Southern Bank of the Thames and its Places of Amusement—Fights between Animals—Edward Alleyn and the Lions—The Watermen and their Poet.

WE have related above how the Burbages, tired of their ground on Finsbury Fields, north of London, pulled down "The Theatre" and removed the materials to Bankside, where they used part of them to build a new theatre.

The southern bank of the Thames was, and is still, called Bankside. Behind the part of it which was covered with buildings there were — to the south of the City—large commons which were used for all kinds of sport—target-shooting in Newington Butts, baiting of wild beasts in the grounds of Paris Garden, etc. There were also large inns where all kinds of amusements went on, and two circuses and amphitheatres, one for bear-baiting and one for bull-baiting, to which the citizens of London frequently made excursions.

In the inhabited part of the south side of London, called Southwark, the acting of plays, and complaints thereof, had been common at an early period.

As early as 1547, the Bishop of Winchester, Stephen Gardiner, complained of the actors' competition with himself. It was intended, he writes in his petition,

4—View of London, with the "Swan," "For[t]

Theatres (from Visscher's View of London, 1616).

which was presented to the Privy Council, to celebrate a solemn funeral mass for the late blessed King Henry VIII. ; but the Southwark actors insisted that they were also going to perform "a solemn play, to try who would get the largest audience, they in play or I in earnest," and the Bishop requests that this blasphemy may be prevented.[1]

The course of theatrical events on the south of the river was exactly the same as on the north.

When the actors were banished from the precincts of the town by the Mayor and Corporation, there could be no question where those who went southward should set up their theatres. Close to the bank, which at this time was covered with one or more rows of houses, stood the two above-mentioned "Rings" for bear and bull-fights, popular amusements which were then, and long continued to be, one of the favourite entertainments of the Londoners, and which were a very characteristic feature of their public life.

In books of travel by strangers who visited London at this time, we look in vain for the name of Shakespeare. Not a line is found even about any of his plays. The bear-fights, on the other hand, seem to have made a deep impression on the minds of the travellers, to judge from the numerous descriptions of them which they have left. Thus one of the attendants of the Spanish ambassador, the Duke of Nájera, writes about a sojourn in London in 1544 :—

"On the other side of the town we saw seven bears, some of them very large ; they are driven into a circus,

---

[1] Related by Ordish after *State Papers, Domestic*, February 5th, 1547.

where they are enclosed by a long rope.   Great fierce
dogs are let loose against them as if to be eaten by them,
and a fight takes place.   It is no bad joke to look at this
fight.   The great bears fight with three or four dogs;
sometimes the former, sometimes the latter, get the upper
hand.   The bears are savage and very strong, and not
only defend themselves with their teeth, but embrace the
dogs so tightly with their forelegs, that these would be
suffocated if they were not helped by their masters.   In
the same place a pony is pushed on with a monkey on
its back, and defends itself against the dogs by kicking
them.   The screams of the monkey in seeing the dogs
hanging on to the ears and neck of the pony make this
scene appear very amusing." [1]

Considering the early period at which this report was
written, we cannot wonder that the Spaniard had nothing
to say about English plays.   It is more astonishing that
in 1598, when the drama and the art of its representation
were in their full glory, the German traveller, Paul
Hentzner, should only have a few lines to devote to
the theatres proper, while he gives the following interesting description of the fights between the animals : " There
is still another place, built in form of a theatre, which
serves for the baiting of bulls and bears; they are
fastened behind, and then worried by great English bull-
dogs, but not without great risque to the dogs, from the
horns of the one and the teeth of the other ; and it sometimes happens they are killed upon the spot ; fresh ones
are immediately supplied in the places of those that are

---

[1] From a Spanish manuscript in the British Museum, quoted by J. P.
Collier: *English Dramatic Poetry*, iii. p. 94.

wounded or tired. To this entertainment there often follows that of a blinded bear, which is performed by five or six men, standing circularly with whips, which they exercise upon him without any mercy, as he cannot escape from them because of his chain ; he defends himself with all his force and skill, throwing down all who come within his reach and are not active enough to get out of it, and tearing the whips out of their hands and breaking them."

Indeed, these excessively brutal sports were not only an amusement to the people : they were also very much relished by the higher classes. In a play by Richard Brome, *The Antipodes* (1638), there is a scene in which an old woman reads a programme of a bear-fight. A young girl warns her against that kind of amusement in the following words : " Let me ask one thing of you. Avoid that kind of animal pastime, it is the work of Satan." But the old woman replies : " Beware what you are saying, child ; *it is the King's delight*." [1]

And it was the Queen's also at that time. When foreign princes visited the English court, it was the fashion to show them the performances of the English dogs ; [1] there was even a special royal functionary, whose business it was to see that there should always be a sufficient supply of animals, so that there might be a performance ready at short notice for Royalty. This office of " Master of the Royal Games of Bears, Bulls and Dogs " was eagerly sought after, among others by

[1] A German report of the visit of the Duke of Würtemberg to a fight between dogs and bears, in 1592, informs us that there were at that time about 120 royal dogs.—Rye : *England as Seen by Foreigners*, p. 45 ; quoted by Ordish, p. 209.

the celebrated actor Edward Alleyn, who indeed finally
succeeded in obtaining it.   No doubt he gained a considerable part of his large fortune by these sports.   One
of the first things which James I. did after his accession
was to assist at a fight between dogs and a lion in the
Tower under the superintendence of Alleyn.   The account
of this, to us, revolting spectacle may be found in John
Stow's " Annales of England " (1603).[1]   As this report
is very little known and throws an interesting light on
the taste of the time, it may not seem unreasonable to
quote it here in spite of its length :—

    " Whereupon the king caused Edward Allen, late
servant to the Lord Admirall, now sworne the Prince's
man and Maister of the Beare Garden, to fetch secretly
three of the fellest dogs in the Garden, which being done,
the King, Queene and Prince with 4 or 5 Lords, went to
the Lions Towre, and caused the lustiest lion to be
separated from his mate, and put into the Lions den one
dog alone, who presently flew to the face of the Lion,
but the Lion suddenly shooke him off, and grasped him
fast by the necke, drawing the dog up staires and downe
staires.   The King now perceiving the Lion greatly to
exceede the dog in strength, but nothing in noble heart
and courage, caused another dog to be put into the den,
who proved as hotte and lusty as his fellow, and tooke the
Lion by the face, but the Lion began to deale with him
as with the former ; whereupon the King commanded
the third dog to be put in before the second dog was
spoiled, which third dog, more fierce and fell than either
of the former, and in despight either of clawes or strength,

[1] It is quoted here from the edition of 1631, pp. 835 f.

tooke the Lyon by the lip, but the Lion so tore the dog by the eyes, head and face, that he lost his hold, and then the Lion took the dog's neck in his mouth, drawing him up and downe as he did the former, but being wearied, could not bite so deadly as the first, now whilest the last dog was thus hand to hand with the Lion in the upper roome, the other two dogs were fighting together in the lower roome, whereupon the King caused the Lion to be driven downe, thinking the lion would have parted them, but when he saw he must needs come by them, he leapt cleane over them both, and contrary to the King's expectation, the lion fled into an inward den, and would not by any means endure the presence of the dogs, albeit the last dogge pursued eagerly, but could not finde the way to the Lion. You shall understand the two last dogs whilest the Lion held them both under his pawes, did bite the Lion by the belly, whereat the Lion roared so extreamely that the earth shooke withall, and the next Lion rampt and roared as if she would have made rescue. The Lion hath not any peculiar or proper kind of fight, as hath the dog, beare or bull, but only a ravenous kinde of surprising for prey. The 2 first dogs dyed within few dayes, but the last dog was well recovered of all his hurts, and the young Prince commanded his servant E. Allen to bring the dog to him to S. James, where the Prince charged the said Allen to keepe him and make much of him, saying, he that had fought with the King of Beasts, should never after fight with any inferior creature."

This strong predilection for exciting fights between

wild beasts, a predilection which in a somewhat modified form still survives in the English nation, drew crowds to the southern bank of the Thames, and made the open parks, the gay riverside and the stately inns favourite places of excursion, especially in summer-time, when the grounds offered the additional attractions of lively strolling musicians, male and female rope-dancers, puppet-shows, clowns who danced the Morris-dance, and fools who sang comic songs. Rare foreign animals were also exhibited, as well as giants, grotesque dwarfs and peculiar mechanical devices.[1]

And behind these places of amusement—on the space now occupied by Lambeth, the most miserable and dirty quarter of London—we find in those times fresh and bright green meadows, with cattle grazing and birds singing. It was a charming place to keep holiday in for all who belonged to "old merry England"; here they might sit down on the turf enjoying the contents of their well-filled hampers—strong beer and savoury meat—and consider which performances were to be visited after the meal, the bear-fight or the rope-dancers, the fencing matches or the comedians.

The principal means of reaching the southern bank was the ferry-boats. Only one bridge crossed the

[1] Shakespeare also testifies to the taste of the time for all monstrous curiosities. In *The Tempest* he makes Trinculo say of Caliban, on meeting this remarkable creature for the first time : " What have we here ? a man or a fish ? dead or alive ? A fish : he smells like a fish ; a very ancient and fish-like smell ; a kind of, not of the newest, poor—John. A strange fish ! Were I in England now, as once I was, and had but this fish painted, not a holiday fool there would but give a piece of silver; there would this monster make a man ; any strange beast there makes a man; when they will not give a doit to relieve a lame beggar, they will lay out ten to see a dead Indian." Act ii. Sc. 2.

Thames within the circuit of the town—old London Bridge, which was thickly covered with houses and towers, full of shops and tradespeople. But along both banks there were a quantity of landing-places, " stairs," between which people were rowed or sculled across by the watermen, a very numerous and rather important corporation of old disbanded seamen, who in times of peace gained their livelihood on the river, while in war-time all who were not disabled had to leave the oar and go out to serve in the Navy again, and fight for the honour of Old England.

The watermen were well aware of their responsible and important task, and their charges were consider- able ;[1] but they were popular, and their busy traffic on the river is a characteristic feature in the physiognomy of London in those days. It is interesting for its close connection with stage matters. In the history of the drama we several times meet with the name of a water- man, Jacob Mead, as theatrical manager, either in co- operation with or in opposition to the great managers, Philip Henslowe and Edward Alleyn. Another, the well-known John Taylor,[2] " the water-poet," as he called himself, was a friend of actors and dramatic authors, took his meals with them in the " Cardinal's Hat " and other public-houses, and even appeared in person on the stage and as an author. Shakespeare, no doubt, many times sat in the ferry-boats of Taylor and his comrades, listening to the tough yarns which were spun there ; and

---

[1] In the very accurate accounts of the actor, Edward Alleyn, I find several times the sum of one shilling put down for a passage by ferry; sometimes, however, only 4d. ; for short passages the fare was 3d.

[2] Sometimes erroneously confounded with the actor Joseph Taylor.

all who have wondered at the great poet's skill in sea-manship, though he is not known to have ever been on the sea, might perhaps have found the source of his knowledge in his familiarity with the able seamen of the Thames.

This John Taylor was a very curious person and very characteristic of his time; originally a mariner, afterwards an invalid, waterman and poet. He made songs to order for weddings and funerals, wrote pamphlets on contemporary people and events, held rhyming tournaments in the play-houses, and undertook the most eccentric "travelling-matches," [1] which he afterwards described in humorous pamphlets. Sometimes also he pleaded as representative of his comrades, the watermen, and on one occasion he throws a light on the state of the ferry traffic to the theatres, which is not without interest. In 1613, at a time when the actors were again beginning to move into the town, in particular deserting Bankside, south of the Thames, the watermen experienced considerable decline in their income, and Taylor sent a petition to the King concerning the actors, to prevent them from keeping a play-house in London on

---

[1] Of these travelling matches, which even now have not quite gone out of fashion in England, one consisted in travelling on foot from London to Edinburgh without a penny in the pocket, and without "begging, borrowing, or asking for meat, drink, or lodging." Another still more eccentric journey was the one he undertook, in company with a vintner, from London to Queenborough. They were to row in a boat of cartridge paper, and with oars made of two stockfishes tied to sticks. However, before they had rowed three miles, the boat came to pieces, and the travellers barely escaped from the venture. John Taylor left in all sixty-three works of great interest to investigators of the life of those times, and all bearing witness to high spirits, though not to a very refined mind. He was born in 1580, and died in 1653.

the northern side of the Thames. He writes in his petition : ". . . Afterwards—the players began to play on *the Bankside*, and to leave playing in London and Middlesex, *for the most part*. Then there went such great concourse of people by water, that the small number of watermen remaining at home were not able to carry them by reason of the court, the tearms, the players, and other employments. So that we were enforced and encouraged, hoping that this golden stirring would have lasted ever, to take and entertaine men and boyes, which boyes are grown men, and keepers of houses ; so that the number of watermen, and those that live and are maintained by them, and by the only labour of the oare and skull, betwixt the bridge of Windsor and Gravesend, cannot be fewer than *forty thousand* ; the cause of the greater halfe of which multitude hath been the players playing on *the Bankside* ; for I have known three companies, besides the bear-baiting, at once there ; to wit, *The Globe*, *The Rose*, and *The Swan*.

" And now it hath pleased God in this peaceful time [from 1604-1613] that there is no employment at the sea, as it hath been accustomed, so that all those great numbers of men remaines at home ; and the players have all (except the King's men) left their usual residence on *the Bankside*, and doe play in Middlesex, far remote from the Thames ; so *that every day in the weeke they do draw unto them three or four thousand people*, that were used to spend their monies by water.

" His Majesties Players did exhibit a petition against us, in which they said, that our suit was unreasonable, and that we might as justly remove the Exchange, the walkes in Paul's or Moorefields, to the Bankside, for our profits, as to confine them." [1]

V

THUS, very naturally—we might say necessarily—the open pleasure-grounds south of the Thames became the next resort of the actors when banished by the Lord Mayor from the precincts of the town itself.

Indeed, we know absolutely nothing about the theatrical matters of the first years after the eviction from Southwark, which also came under the jurisdiction of the Lord Mayor. Whether, immediately after the establishment of "The Theatre" and "The Curtain," a permanent play-house was built on the Southside, we do not know; but, judging from the success of the two northern theatres, it is probable that an attempt was made here also, and it is generally supposed that Newington Butts was the site of the third London theatre.

Our knowledge of stage-matters on the Southside is chiefly derived from "Henslowe's Diary," an account-book kept by the stage-manager, Philip Henslowe, during the years 1592 to 1609, the manuscript of which was found about a hundred years ago by the excellent Shake-

[1] John Taylor: *Works*, edit. 1633, p. 171; quoted by Malone: *Historical Account*, p. 164, n. 7.

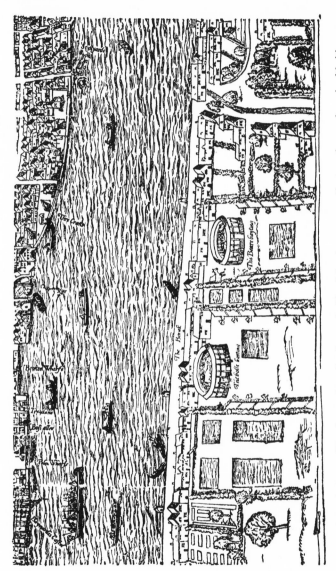

The Banck

This Beare bayting

Nicholls Fortau

5—Part of a Map of London, 1560.   On the south side of the river are seen the two circuses for animal-baiting.

spearean archæologist, Edmond Malone,[1] in Dulwich College, founded by Edward Alleyn, the son-in-law of Henslowe.

Like his contemporary, James Burbage, Henslowe, the builder of " The Theatre," was originally an artisan, by occupation a dyer. But there is nothing to show that he ever practised the dramatic art in person. It is still less probable that he was a dramatic author, for his accounts and letters bear witness of the most helpless ignorance of the art of writing, and his orthography is, even for those times, quite puzzling in its absurd irregularity.[2] But if he was not a literary man, he was certainly a man of business. It appears, to judge from the Diary,[3] that from 1577 to 1578 he occupied himself with forest exploitation and the timber trade. It is difficult to say whether about that period he had already begun his theatrical enterprises. His theatrical accounts do not begin till 1592, but before that time there are entries which prove that he lent money on interest, a transaction which he continued assiduously to the end of his life, and by which he acquired considerable power over the actors in his service.

On October 22nd, 1592, we find the entry in Hens-

---

[1] Malone printed parts of the Diary in an appendix to his *Historical Account of the Rise and Progress of the English Stage*, Basil, MDCCC. Later, in 1845, the whole manuscript was published by J. P. Collier for the Shakespeare Society.

[2] He writes, for instance, " Troyeless and creasseday" for *Troilus and Cressida*; "titus and ondronicous" for *Titus Andronicus*; "the venesyon comodey" for *The Venetian Comedy*; " Doctor Fostose" for *Doctor Faustus*; "sesor and pompie" for *Cæsar and Pompey*, etc. Comp. *Henslowe's Diary*, edited by Collier, pp. 149, 33, 41, 42 and 44.

[3] Collier questions whether this part of the Diary is Henslowe's own, but this has been established beyond doubt by G. F. Warner (*Catalogue of MSS. and Monuments of Alleyn's College of Gods Gift at Dulwich*, 1881, p. 157).

lowe's Diary : " Edward Alleyn was wedded to Jone Woodward." Though it is more than probable that Henslowe had been interested in theatrical business for some years before that time, this short note nevertheless marks a turning point in his dramatic career. Joan Woodward was his step-daughter, and her husband was one of the most distinguished actors of his time, and perhaps the most active theatrical manager of whom this epoch can boast. This close family connection with the popular actor no doubt strengthened Henslowe's resolution to build an entirely new theatre, based on the artistic and financial skill of his son-in-law, and this plan was carried out in the same year, 1592, when " The Rose " Theatre was built on a piece of ground behind the houses for bear-baiting and bull-baiting on Bankside, and close to the much frequented landing-place of Paris Garden on the Thames.[1]

From the very detailed accounts which Henslowe kept of his expenses for the new theatre, it appears that, like the former play-houses, " The Rose " was chiefly built of wood, that it had turned pillars to support the galleries,[2] and that it was thatched with straw or reeds.[3]

About 1593, therefore, London possessed four per-

[1] The theatre is seen distinctly in Norden's map of London of 1593. It does not follow with absolute certainty from the Diary that " The Rose " theatre was built precisely in 1592, as the account does not give the name of the play-house, but only mentions it as "my play howsse," and it is not stated whether the item relates to repairs or a new building. But it seems most probable that the new " Rose " Theatre was meant. Comp. this item with a later one of 1595, which relates to repairs.—See *Henslowe's Diary*, pp. 11-15 and p. 4.

[2] As we see also in the somewhat later " Swan " Theatre in the illustration of the interior, discovered by Dr Gaedertz.—Gaedertz : *Zur Kenntniss der altenglischen Bühne*, etc.

[3] In the accounts are found several items for the thatcher and his men.

manent play-houses; two on the north side, "The Theatre" and "The Curtain," and two on the south side, "Newington Butts" and "The Rose," all four, however, outside the proper territory of the town. Things had developed in a remarkably similar way on both sides of the Thames; two plain and quite illiterate master-workmen, a joiner and a dyer, each build or invest money in two theatres, and create incomes for themselves by levying contributions on the acting companies to whom they let their stages.

There was no arrangement confining each company to its own stage. On the contrary, we see from Henslowe's "Diary" that now one, now another company appeared on his stage, and that he charged them different rents. Burbage's actors played on Henslowe's stage, and the reverse may also have been the case, though this is not proved.

The company, however, which was more particularly attached to Henslowe's enterprise was that of "The Lord Admiral's Men," a company of which Henslowe's son-in-law, Edward Alleyn, became the stage director, and unquestionably the leading actor. We can scarcely be mistaken in assuming that during the earliest period of permanent theatres "The Lord Admiral's Men" were the leading company in London. It was for them, above all, that Christopher Marlowe, the greatest dramatic author before Shakespeare, shone forth and wrote his plays, in which he probably acted as well, and that Alleyn interpreted before an admiring audience his wild and powerful characters, Tamburlaine, Barabbas (in *The Jew of Malta*), and Dr Faustus.

Noted dramatists, like Thomas Lodge and Thomas Dekker, added to the répertoire of the same company.

However, the increasing fame of Shakespeare as an author, and of Richard Burbage as an actor, soon turned the scales in favour of "The Lord Chamberlain's Servants," to whom these two magnates devoted their life-long work. At the same time, "The Lord Admiral's Men" long continued to maintain their position as the second of the companies.

A paragraph in Henslowe's "Diary" shows us the Lord Chamberlain's and the Lord Admiral's men acting together in brotherly union at Newington Butts. The old manager notes this event in the history of the stage in the following words :—

"In the name of God Amen, beginninge at Newington, my Lord Admiralle and my Lorde chamberlen men, as followeth, 1594."[1]

After which, as usual, he puts down the share he has received for each day of performance and for each play. We see that he gets very little, much less than his usual share—it varies between 17s. and 4s., while on other occasions he frequently receives several pounds.

[1] I happen to notice that Mr Sidney Lee, in his new, large, and excellent biography of Shakespeare (*A Life of William Shakespeare*, illustrated library edition, 1899, p. 35) mentions this joint acting of the companies as having taken place in 1592 in "The Rose" Theatre, and as having lasted for "some months," and that on the same page he confuses some data relating to the history of the stage. Otherwise, Mr Lee's book is well known for its sound accuracy, and in this respect compares favourably with the numerous æsthetical appreciations of Shakespeare, in which theatrical matters are nearly always neglected. I do not write this note in order to correct the distinguished English author, but merely as a kind of anticipatory apology for possible mistakes which I may happen to commit. Where even the greatest experts can err, it will easily be understood that the ground is difficult and not much worked.

This, perhaps, is the reason why the partnership lasted so short a time, only ten days, from June 3rd to 13th. Possibly the shares, having to be divided between so many distinguished persons, became too small for the money-loving Henslowe; possibly it was simply a case of a rupture. This, at any rate, is certain, that we never afterwards hear of a co-operation between the two companies; the name of Shakespeare is not even mentioned in the papers left either by Henslowe or by Alleyn.[1]

The competition between the two leading companies reached its height when " The Lord Chamberlain's Men " definitely left the Shoreditch quarter and settled on Bankside.

We have seen how Richard Burbage and his companions, no doubt including Shakespeare, on a day in 1598[2] pulled down their old " Theatre " and removed the timber to Bankside. There, in the immediate vicinity of " The Rose " and " The Bear-garden," they made their builder, the carpenter Peter Street, erect a new play-house, which they decorated with a splendid sign which, according to the fashion of the time, was painted on the outer wall. It represented Atlas[3] carrying the globe, and underneath was written " *Totus mundus agit histrionem.*" The new play-house was no doubt finished in the

---

[1] In the *Alleyn Papers* and *Memoirs of Alleyn*, indeed, published by J. P. Collier, we find Shakespeare occasionally mentioned; but these passages are only some of the editor's frequent forgeries, detected too late.

[2] Not in 1593 as stated by Collier.

[3] In the literature of the time, and even in modern writings on Shakespeare, Hercules is generally charged with this heavy task, though it justly devolves on Atlas. Comp, for instance, *Hamlet, ii.* 2 ("Hercules and his burden," even in speaking about "The Globe.") Malone's *Historical Account*, p. 69, and Collier, *English Dramatic Poetry*, iii. p. 113.

same year in which it had been commenced, at any rate in 1599, and after its sign it was called " The Globe."

There are several illustrations of " The Globe " Theatre—among others that reproduced here from Visscher's " View of London " (fig. 4)—and we should like to think that the theatre, the octagonal exterior of which is so well known, was identical with that to which Shakespeare was attached, for which he wrote his best plays, and where he made his money.

This, however, is not so. There is no picture of Shakespeare's " Globe," and we know scarcely anything about its outward appearance. In 1613, shortly after Shakespeare had retired, the play-house built by Richard Burbage was destroyed by fire ; a new one, more suitable to the requirements of the time, rose in its place, and this is the building we see represented in the familiar drawings.

The original " Globe " was constructed—as already mentioned—of the material of " The Theatre," which had been pulled down. No doubt, like the latter, it was circular in shape. This seems to be proved by Shakespeare's words in the prologue of one of the first plays which was acted on its stage, viz. in *Henry the Fifth*, where we read :—

> " . . . Can this cockpit hold
> The vasty fields of France ? or may we cram
> Within this wooden O, the very casques
> That did affright the air at Agincourt ? "

It is possible, indeed, that only the inside of the building was circular while the outside was polygonal, but

there is no proof that it was so, and there is more pro-
bability in favour of the circular form.[1]

That the first "Globe" was of wood, we gather not
only from this prologue, but also from the above story of
the removal of its material, and from other evidence as
well. The roof was thatched, and the whole house was
probably neither very large nor very splendid. Other
qualities than outward stateliness made "The Globe"
what it became during this short period before it was
burned down; the workshop where the most precious
jewels of English literature were produced.

During these years, from 1599 to 1613, masterpiece
after masterpiece was represented on this plain wooden
platform, "this unworthy scaffold," as the poet himself
calls his stage.[2]

Henry V. had already secured the success of the new
theatre. This play, indeed, was not one of the master-
pieces, but it dealt with the most popular national hero
of the English, and served as a patriotic *clou* which
neither could nor did miss its effect, the victory of the
English over the French at Agincourt. Too modestly
Shakespeare says about the performance :—

". . . And so our scene must to the battle fly ;
Where (O for pity !) we shall much disgrace—
With four or five most vile and ragged foils
Right ill disposed in brawl ridiculous,—

[1] A passage in Heywood's *Apology for Actors* (Shakespeare Society's
Reprint, London, 1841, p. 37) also seems to prove the circular shape of the
ancient "Globe." He speaks of the Roman circuses and supposes them to
have differed in shape from theatres and amphitheatres, their frame having
been "*globe*-like and merely *round*." Heywood's *Apology* appeared while
the ancient "Globe" still existed, namely in 1612.

[2] *Henry V.*, prologue to Act iv.

The name of Agincourt : Yet sit and see ;
Minding true things by what their mockeries be."

Even though a representation on the stage must necessarily be far removed from the picturesque splendour of reality—a circumstance, by the by, which the prologues of this play constantly impress upon us—we may be sure that nothing was neglected to reproduce a battle scene as magnificently as possible at a period when fighting on the stage was so common and so popular.

This play, at any rate, was a marvellous success, and was followed by others which better deserved to be so. First came a series of splendid comedies, like *Much Ado About Nothing*, in which the celebrated comic actor, William Kemp, delighted the public as the ingenious constable Dogberry ; *The Merry Wives of Windsor*, no doubt with John Heminge as Sir John Falstaff (brought to life again by order of the Queen) ; *As You Like It* and *Twelfth Night*, in which Malvolio won special popularity as a caricature of the sour and conceited Puritans.

Then followed such achievements as *Julius Cæsar* (1600 or 1601), *Hamlet* (1601 or 1602), *Othello* (1604), *King Lear* (1605), *Macbeth* (1606), *Timon of Athens* (1606), *Antony and Cleopatra* (1607), *Coriolanus* (1608), *Cymbeline* (1609), *A Winter's Tale* (1610), *The Tempest* [1] (1610) ; all produced with Richard Burbage in the principal parts.   The same period saw Ben Jonson's *Sejanus*

---

[1] The year of performance of some of the plays is perforce only given approximately.   I am chiefly guided by Fleay (*Chronicle of the English Drama*).   The last pieces—after 1608—may possibly have been acted at Blackfriars as well.

(1603), *Volpone* (1605), *The Alchymist* (1610), and *The Conspiracy of Catilina* (1611); and Beaumont and Fletcher's *Philaster*.

VI

Building of " The Fortune " Theatre—Its Situation and Arrangement—
Difficulties and Dangers threatening from the Authorities.

As a matter of course, a theatre with such cards in its hand as " The Globe " attracted great attention from the public. Indeed Henslowe and Alleyn seem to have understood at once that competition with Burbage's excellent company was out of the question.

Still they did not give up, and they had no reason to do so. They were part-owners of " The Bear-garden," the arena for bear-fights which has been repeatedly mentioned, and they made much money by it. Later, as already stated, they succeeded in obtaining after several vain attempts the eagerly desired patent as " Masters of the Royal Games," a function which gave them very great advantages. In short, they were very wealthy men.

On seeing that the fame of " The Rose " Theatre was bound to decline in the immediate vicinity of the new and rising " Globe," they did not hesitate to leave it to its fate, and to build a new play-house in a new quarter. Thither Alleyn went with his company, " The Lord Admiral's Men," [1] while " The Rose " was let to companies of minor importance.

[1] They were also called " The Earl of Nottingham's Men," and were under the patronage of Lord Charles Howard, until at the accession of King James (1603) they were given the title of " The Prince's (Henry's) Servants."

Before this, a somewhat inferior company called
" Lord Sussex's Men " had played here ; now Henslowe
let the building to " The Earl of Worcester's Players,"
who afterwards, in 1603, became "The Queen's (*i.e.*
Anne of Denmark's) Men." This company, however,
does not seem to have been successful there, and after
1603 we hear very little of " The Rose " Theatre.
Apparently it sank to a lower class of performances—
puppet-shows and displays of fighting.   On Visscher's
map of London of 1616, we find no trace of this theatre.
At that time, therefore, it had very likely been pulled
down.   " Rose Alley," [1] the name of a street, still exists
as a reminder of Henslowe's old play-house.

As early as the year after " The Globe" had been
built, on January 8th, 1600, Henslowe and Alleyn made
a contract with Peter Street, who had built for Burbage,
for the construction of a new, large and fashionable
theatre on a site which the two managers had acquired
in St Giles's Parish near Golden Lane and outside
Cripplegate.   They moved, that is, to the north of the
town, far away from Burbage and his dangerous competition, but though the ground chosen lay outside the
gate, and was consequently safe from the persecution
of the Mayor and Corporation, it was still in a densely
crowded and much frequented quarter.

As we learn from the builder's contract,[2] this new
play-house was to be something hitherto unknown in
shape, size and solidity.   In contrast to the earlier
theatres, which had only been of wood, it had a founda-

---

[1] T. F. Ordish : *Early London Theatres*, p. 200.
[2] Published *in extenso* in Halliwell-Phillipps's *Outlines*, 3rd ed., pp. 524 ff.

tion of brick, which was to rise a foot above the ground; in shape it was square, while the former theatres were circular; its dimensions were spacious for those times, for it measured 80 feet each way outside, and 55 feet inside. It was built with three storeys, the lowest 12 feet high, the middle 11, and the upper 9. Each storey was 12 feet deep; the floor of each of the two upper galleries protruded 12 inches. There were four sets of "Gentlemen rooms"—the best seats, a sufficient number of "twopenny rooms" for the middle class, and seats in every part of the galleries. The stairs, passages and partitions were to be similar to those which Peter Strange had made in "The Globe," the newly-built play-house on Bankside. This piece of information, however, does not make us any the wiser with regard to the construction of the Shakespearean theatre. On the whole this contract does *not*—as Halliwell-Phillipps and others think —tell us what "The Globe" was like; it merely states all the points in which Henslowe's new theatre was to differ from it.

The stage was to be 43 feet broad, and its length was to extend to the middle of the pit (the yard[1]), being supported below by strong new oak planks. Above it was to be placed a roof covered with tiles like the galleries and the tiring-house, and provided with leaden gutters so arranged as to let the water out at the back— not over the stage or the spectators. In all other respects the stage was to be arranged like that of " The Globe,"

---

[1] The contract says the reverse, but evidently the meaning must be as stated above, as elsewhere in the contract the word breadth is used for what we should call depth. By length I here understand the distance from the tiring-room to the end of the platform.

with suitable windows and glass panes in the tiring-house. No windows are mentioned in the auditorium, and there probably were none, as the galleries were open towards the yard or pit.

" And the saide howse," the contract continues, " and other thinges before mentioned to be made and doen, to be in all other contrivitions, conveyances, fashions, thinge and thinges, effected, finished and doen, according to the manner and fashion of the saide house called the Globe ; saveinge only that all the principall and maine postes of the saide frame and stadge forward shall be square and wrought palaster-wise, with carved proportions called satiers to be placed and sett on the topp of every of the same postes ; and saveing also that the same Peter Streete shall not be charged with anie manner of paynteinge in or about the saide frame, howse or stadge, or anie parte thereof, etc."

Street was desired to use timber of larger dimensions and heavier weight than that which had been employed in " The Globe," and his payment for the building was £440.

The entire sum, however, for the complete structure with the decorations and painting was £520, as appears from an entry in one of Edward Alleyn's note-books, where we read :—

" What ' The Fortune ' cost me, Nov. 1599 :—

" First for the leas to Brew [1]   .   . £240

" Then for building the playhous   .   520

" For other privat buildings of myn owne   120

" So that it hath cost me for the lease . £880 "

[1] Patrick Brew, a goldsmith in Lombard Street. Among the *Alleyn Papers* there are several letters to and from him. J. P. Collier in his

In front of the theatre was placed a painted statue of the Goddess of Fortune, and the house was called after her, " The Fortune." [1]

The new theatre had probably been opened by the beginning of the following year (1601). In August, at any rate, we find it in full activity, for at that date Henslowe had to pay three pounds in taxes for the past month [2] to the Master of the Revels.

But even before the building was finished, the expectations as to this large new theatre had caused a great sensation in London, and called forth fresh complaints from the Puritans, complaints which this time threatened to break in a violent storm on the heads of the actors.

On account of these complaints the Lords of the Privy Council felt bound, on the 22nd of June 1600, to issue an order that in future there must be only two theatres in London. The Privy Council considers " the exercise of such playes not beinge esvill in ytself, may with good order and moderation be suffered in a well-governed state," especially as " her Majestie, beinge

---

English Dramatic Poetry, iii. 119, calls him Drew, and does not seem to know who he is ; which is all the more remarkable because it was Collier himself who discovered and published the letters in the *Alleyn Papers*.

[1] In Thomas Heywood's *The English Traveller* (iv. 6) we read :

> " I'll rather stand here
> Like a statue in the forefront of your house
> For ever—like the picture of dame Fortune
> Before the Fortune Play-house."

It is possible, however, that this refers to the rebuilt " Fortuna," in 1623, and that the previous one had to content itself with a painted sign like " The Globe." *The English Traveller* appeared in 1633, but the date of its performance is unknown.

[2] Henslowe's *Diary*, p. 182.

pleased at tymes to take delight and recreation in the sight and hearinge of them."

It was not expedient, therefore, to suppress them entirely. But, on the other hand, it was notorious that "the multitude of the saide houses and the mysgovernment hath been and is dayly occasion of the ydle, ryotous and dissolute living of great nombers of people, that, leavinge all such honest and painefull course of life as they should followe, doe meete and assemble there."

So the Council had to decide that in future there must only be two play-houses in or near London, one on Bankside and one in the county of Middlesex. But meanwhile their lordships had learned from the Master of the Revels, Sir Edmund Tylney, who received large gratuities from Henslowe and Alleyn, "that the house nowe in hand to be builte by the saide Edward Allen is not intended to increase the nomber of the playhouses, but to be insteede of another, namely the Curtayne, which is either to be ruined and plucked downe or to be put to some other good use."[1] Therefore, and because its situation was altogether suitable for its purpose, Alleyn's house was allowed to be one of the two acknowledged theatres, the one in Middlesex, and " The Lord Admiral's Servants" were permitted to act there. The other, that on the Surrey side or Bankside, was to be " The Globe," where " The Lord Chamberlain's Men" were allowed to perform.

But in no other places in or out of London were plays to be performed, and it was specially forbidden

[1] Halliwell-Phillipps : *Outlines*, p. 530.

"that any stage-playes shall be played, as sometymes they have bin, in any common inne for publique assembly in or neare about the Cittie."

Further, the two privileged companies were not to play more than twice a week, " each of them in their severall house twice a weeke and no oftener, and especially they shall refrayne to play on the Sabbath day upon payne of imprysonment and further penaltie."

Finally—" because these orders wil be of little force and effecte unlesse they be duely putt in execution by those unto whome it appertayneth to see them executed, it is ordered that severall copies of these orders shal be sent to the Lord Maior of London and to the Justices of Peace of the counties of Middlesex and Surrey, and that letters shal be written unto them from their Lordships straightly chargeinge them to see to the execution of the same, as well by commyttinge to prison any owners of playhouses and players as shall disobey and resist these orders as by any other good and lawfull means that in their discretion they shall finde expedient, and to certifie their Lordships from tyme to tyme as they shall see cause of their proceedinges heerein." [1]

At that moment there were at least six permanent theatres in London. The Burbages possessed two, " The Globe" and " The Blackfriars"; Henslowe and Alleyn three, " The Rose," " The Fortune," and " The Curtain," the last of which they must have acquired by

----

[1] This order from the Privy Council, with certain other documents concerning the same affair, is reproduced *in extenso* in Halliwell-Phillipps's *Outlines*, 3rd ed., pp. 528-535.

this time, since they promise to pull it down when they build "The Fortune"; finally there was a sixth belonging to a certain Francis Langley, "The Swan," the history of which we shall soon have an opportunity of relating. It may be also that "The Newington" Theatre still existed, but it was of scarcely any importance, and its whole history is very obscure.

At any rate the strict orders from the Privy Council meant the suppression of four large play-houses, three of which were only a few years old.

Fortunately for the actors and the proprietors, this order shared the fate of many others: it was never carried out. A year and a half later, in December 1601, the Lord Mayor sends in a new complaint of the many theatres, to which the Privy Council replies as follows: " Wee have receaved a lettre from yow renewing a complaint of the great abuse and disorder within and about the cittie of London by reason of the multitude of playhowses, . . . wee must let yow know that wee did much rather expect to understand that our order sett downe and prescribed about a yeare and a half since for reformation of the said disorders upon the lyke complaint at that tyme had been duely executed, then to finde the same disorders and abuses so muche encreased as they are. The blame whereof, as we cannot but impute in great part to the Justices of the Peace or some of them in the counties of Middlesex and Surrey, who had speciall direction and charge from us to see our said Order executed for the confines of the Cittie, wherein the most part of those play-howses are scituate. . . . Wee do therefore once againe renew hereby our directions unto you, as wee have donne by our lettres to the justices of Middlesex and Surrey. . . ."[1]

Here follows a repetition of the earlier order, which winds up with a request to imprison the proprietors of theatres if, regardless of their duty, they have plays acted in other places besides the two authorised theatres, "The Fortune" and "The Globe." And, as before, a strict injunction is sent to the Justices of the Peace.

But, just as before, the writs were entirely disregarded. It is most astonishing to see how such orders from the highest authorities are ignored time after time, and treated as empty menaces in spite of their being addressed to the Puritan Lord Mayor, the hereditary enemy of actors.

This would be quite incomprehensible if the Lords of the Council had not played a double game, secretly protecting the theatres while publicly censuring them. Among the councillors of state at that time were men like Nottingham, Shrewsbury and Worcester, who were known to be very favourably inclined towards plays and actors, and who, without openly breaking with the Mayor and the Corporation, found it amusing to play a few tricks on the conceited Puritan prigs.

That the actors also considered the grave city fathers as a good butt for their wit is seen for one thing from the almost farcical way in which Shakespeare treats the Lord Mayor and Aldermen in his *Richard III.*, where he makes Gloster and Buckingham send them off on a

[1] The county of Middlesex contained the part of London which lay north of the Thames, the county of Surrey contained the part south of the river.

wild goose chace, and exhibits them as foolish victims of the grossest dissimulation.

At any rate, the theatres were left alone for the present. It is true that the proprietors had to pay a considerable sum to the functionaries in whose hands their welfare lay, and we shall see later how the Master of the Revels taxed the actors. Still, the theatres which had to succumb in the struggle for existence perished by a natural death, and no brute force was exercised against their development.

Not even " The Curtain " disappeared, though Henslowe and Alleyn had engaged themselves to pull it down when they built " The Fortune." It continued to exist, as we have seen, probably down to the time of the Civil War. It is even possible that Henslowe and Alleyn never owned this theatre, in which case, indeed, the promise of pulling it down would be the climax of comic impudence to the Puritan authorities. This promise, as far as I know, is the only indication of " The Curtain's " ever having been in the possession of Henslowe and Alleyn. In their detailed account-books no mention whatever is made of it.

But a few years previously the two partners had built " The Rose," which, indeed, they did not show the slightest intention of pulling down. On the whole, the last twenty or thirty years of the century had brought vigorous life into the theatrical world, and, it must be confessed, had increased the number of theatres slightly beyond what the town was able to support at the time.

About the year 1596 a large new play-house had been added, of which we have not yet had an opportunity of speaking in greater detail. It was called "The Swan," and like "The Rose" and "The Globe," it was situated on the southern bank of the Thames, but more to the west than the others.

A Dutch scholar, Johan de Witt, who visited London about that time, has left not only a description but also a drawing [1] of this theatre, which in 1596 was quite new, and for that very reason, perhaps, particularly impressed the foreign traveller by its stately appearance. The translation of his Latin description runs as follows: "There are in London four theatres (*Amphitheatra*) of noteworthy beauty, which bear different names according to their different signs. In each of them a different play (*varia scœna*) is daily performed before the people. The two most magnificent of these are situated across the Thames on the south side, and are called from the signs suspended over them: 'The Rose' [2] and 'The Swan.' Two others, 'The Theatre' and 'The Curtain,' are situated outside the town to the north, on the road which is entered through 'the episcopal gate,' generally called 'Bishopsgate.' There is also a fifth, but of a different construction, meant for baiting of wild beasts, in which many bears, bulls and dogs of an extraordinary size are fed in separate dens and cages, which are baited to fight, and thus afford a most delightful spectacle to the people. Of all the theatres the largest and most magnificent is the one whose sign is a Swan (generally called 'The Swan' Theatre), as it holds three thousand persons, and

---

[1] Both were discovered by Dr K. Th. Gaedertz, who found them in the Utrecht Library. The descriptions in the text are taken from his work before mentioned.

[2] "The Rose," as we have seen, was also new at the time.

is built of flint, of which there is a large abundance in England, supported by wooden pillars. The paint that covers these pillars produces such an excellent imitation of marble that it baffles even the sharpest eye. And as in shape it seems to be an imitation of Roman work, I have given a drawing of it above." [1]

This "Swan Theatre," the magnificence of which made such a deep impression on the Dutch scholar, is well known to us from other sources. In the year 1594 the Lord Mayor of London wrote to the Lord Treasurer, informing him that a certain Francis Langley, licensed alnager,[2] intended to build a new theatre on the Bank side, which he asked him to forbid his doing.

Evidently the Lord Treasurer did not comply with the request of the Lord Mayor, for Francis Langley built his theatre on the ground of Paris Garden, quite close to the Bear-garden, and to the much frequented landing-place on the Thames, Paris Gardens Stairs ; and probably from the many swans which crowded the river at the time—he chose a swan as the sign of his play-house, and called it "The Swan Theatre."   There is no evidence to show when "The Swan" was built and opened for use.   If Dr Gaedertz is right in his assertion that de Witt visited London in the summer of 1596, it is not likely to have been open for less than a year. But other circumstances seem to indicate that it was quite new in 1598.[3]

In other respects we are exceedingly well informed

---

[1] The drawing is reproduced in vol. ii. of the present work : Middle Ages and Renaissance, facing p. 326.

[2] Comp. Ordish : *Early London Theatres*, p. 253.

[3] Comp. Ordish : *Early London Theatres*, p. 259.

with regard to this play-house. We possess a drawing of the interior by de Witt; its exterior is illustrated in Visscher's "View of London" (of 1616); it is described, as above, by de Witt, and, finally, we have the fairly detailed building contract of the later "Hope Theatre," the construction of which was to be exactly like that of "The Swan."

This play-house, therefore, as far as its outward history is concerned, is probably the best known of all contemporary theatres. Unfortunately, its importance to the dramatic art and dramatic literature of the time was obviously slight; in any case its artistic history is as obscure as our knowledge of its architecture is clear. It is evident that the builder, Francis Langley, who seems to have selected the place for his fine theatre very judiciously, could not come up to his shrewd competitor, Philip Henslowe, who owned "The Rose," "The Newington" and "The Bear-garden."

When de Witt's drawing appeared, it was thought for a moment that the three actors represented there might be meant for Malvolio, Olivia and Maria in *Twelfth Night*, and that this would prove that Shakespeare had written also for "The Swan" Theatre. But this hypothesis failed on the simple ground that that comedy cannot have been written before 1600.[1] On the whole, there is nothing to justify the belief that any play of Shakespeare's was acted at "The Swan," or that the company to which the great poet belonged, and for which

---

[1] They might, by the by, be the same persons from an earlier play on the same subject. Some people consider *Twelfth Night* to be an adaptation of an earlier comedy.

he wrote exclusively,[1] ever appeared on Langley's stage.

From a short colloquy in Dekker's *Satiromastix* we may conclude that Ben Jonson, whose restless nature drove him in turn to all companies and all theatres, acted Zulziman in "The Swan" Theatre. Otherwise this theatre seems mainly to have been used for performances of a lower kind, the so-called "activities," or what we should call "music hall entertainments," acrobatic tricks, fencing matches, and plays of the lowest class. The once magnificent building soon fell into decay, and, on the whole, this theatrical enterprise seems to have been a failure. In the year 1632, in a play by Marmyon, called *Holland's Leaguer*,[2] after a house of ill fame in Paris Garden, mention is made of the things worth seeing in that neighbourhood, among which occurs "The Swan." The passage runs as follows: "There are pleasant walks and a concourse of strangers. Three famous amphitheatres can be seen from the turret; one, the continent of the world [*i.e.* 'The Globe'], to which half the year [*i.e.* in summer] a world of beauties and of brave spirits resort—a building of excellent Hope for players, wild beasts and gladiators—and one other, that the lady of the leaguer or fortress could almost shake

[1] The only two of Shakespeare's plays which seem to have been written for other companies are *Titus Andronicus*, which we find mentioned in Henslowe's *Diary* (p. 33) as having been performed for the first time on the 23rd of January 1593 or 1594 by the inferior company, "The Earl of Sussex's Men" (Rd at titus and ondronicous, the 23rd of Jeneway . . . iii. li viii. s.), and *Henry VI.*, which on the title-page of the first edition is stated to have been acted by "The Earl of Pembroke's Servants." But as we know, Shakespeare's authorship of both these plays has been contested.

[2] Shakerly Marmyon: *Holland's Leaguer*, 1632; quot. by Ordish: *Early London Theatres*, p. 275.

hands with, now fallen to decay, and, like a dying swanne [*i.e.* 'The Swan' play-house], hangs her head and sings her own dirge."

This melancholy description is the last information we have about the once proud "Swan."

VII

The Burning of "The Globe"—The new "Globe" and its Proprietors—Philip Henslowe as Theatrical Manager—The Burning and Reconstruction of "The Fortune."

On the 29th of June 1613 London saw for the first time the destruction by fire of one of its theatres, and it was no other than "The Globe" which was destroyed.

By this time it was more than a year since Shakespeare had retired from the stage. But a new play in which he had a share was acted on this fatal day. The historical play *Henry VIII.*, or *All is True*, by Shakespeare and Fletcher,[1] was on the play-bill, and this royal drama was produced with much pomp and splendour. The Knights of the Garter appeared in their magnificent robes, and the Knights of St George in theirs ; the Royal Guard were refulgent in their embroidered surcoats ; even the stage—contrary to custom—was covered with mats, while for ordinary use it was only strewn with rushes.

In Act i., Scene 4, the King comes as one of a company of maskers to the house of Cardinal Wolsey, and, in accordance with a common custom, on the entrance of the King a volley of cannon-shots was fired. The wad of one of these hit the roof, and in a twinkling

[1] *Henry VIII.* is supposed to have been commenced by Shakespeare in 1611, and to have been performed two years later by "The King's Men," who had prevailed on Fletcher to finish it.

the sixteen years' old theatre, which, as we remember, was built of wood, was in flames. Though there were only two narrow entrances to the whole theatre, all the people escaped almost unhurt. " Only one man," says the writer of a contemporary letter,[1] " had his breeches set on fire, that would perhaps have broyled him, if he had not by the benefit of a provident wit, put it out with bottle ale."

But the whole theatre and an adjoining house were burned down in a little over an hour, and of course among other things part of the expensive wardrobe of the actors was destroyed.

Naturally the fire created a considerable sensation. The Puritans considered it as a judgment from God,[2] and a street song appeared, which in graphic words, though in a humorous way, preserved the memory of the sad event.

The song has the following title : " A Sonnet about the Sad Fire in the Globe Theatre in London " ;[3] and with an obvious allusion to the piece which was acted on the fatal day, each verse ended with this refrain :—

" Oh, sorrow, pittifull sorrow, an yett all this is true."

[1] Sir Henry Wotton. In *Reliquiæ Wottonianæ*, ed. 1685, pp. 425-6, we find a description of the fire, first quoted by Malone, p. 69, n. 6. A letter from Mr Chamberlain, dated July 8th, 1613, also discovered by Malone (*ibid.*), and Stow's *Chronicle*, under the year 1613, also give descriptions of this event in the annals of the theatre. The details given above are drawn from these three sources.

[2] As late as twenty years after, Prynne, in his *Histriomastix*, mentions the burning of the two theatres, "The Globe" and "The Fortune," as a proof that plays are the work of the devil. See the original edition of 1633, p. 516.

[3] Printed for the first time in *The Gentlemen's Magazine* of 1816, from an old manuscript. Afterwards reprinted by Halliwell-Phillipps (*Outlines*, pp. 536 ff.) Malone mentions a ballad on the same subject, which is registered in the bookseller's catalogue of 1613, but which he has never been able to find. It can scarcely be the same as the above-mentioned sonnet ; the title at least is different.

The sonnet begins in a high strain with a summons to Melpomene to report the last tragedy which was acted at "The Globe."

> " Now sitt the downe, Melpomene,
>   Wrapt in a sea-cole robe,
>   And tell the dolefull tragedie
>   That late was playd at Globe."

Then it describes how the fire began on the roof and spread over the whole house consuming everything, even the silk flag; further, how the knights and noblemen ran out in great confusion, losing their hats and swords, and the actors likewise, Burbage, Condell and old Heminge, who stood with swollen eyes " like a drunken Flemming," and looked with sorrow at the burning wigs, costumes and drum-skins. At last the poet recommends the actors not to thatch their house, but to go to the expense of a tile roof.

> " Be warned, yow stage strutters all,
>   Least yow againe be catched,
>   And such a burneing doe befall,
>   As to them whose howse was thatched ;
>   Forbeare your whoreing, breeding biles,
>   And lay up that expence for tiles.
>   Oh, sorrow, pittifull sorrow, and yet all this is true."

To this warning Burbage and his companions paid heed, and when, as early as the following spring,[1] " The

---

[1] " . . . and the next spring it was new builded in far fairer manner than before."—Stow's *Chronicle*, under the year 1613.

> " As gold is better that's in fire tried,
>   So is the Bankside Globe that late was burn'd,
>   For where before it had a thatched hide,

Globe" rose again, it was not only much more splendid in appearance, but it had a tiled roof.

The new "Globe" remained under the management of Richard Burbage till his death in 1619. After this event it continued to remain in the hands of the family, though now, as before, they shared the ownership with some of the leading actors as partners. No doubt, even on the establishment of the first "Globe Theatre," Shakespeare and others had shares in the enterprise.[1] The bookseller, Cuthbert Burbage, the surviving brother of Richard, writes in the year 1635 on this question, after mentioning the difficulties which the family had had with their first enterprise, "The Theatre": "We then bethought us of altering from thence, and at like expense built the Globe, with more summes of money taken up at *interest, which lay heavy* on us many yeares, and to ourselves wee joyned those deserving men, Shakspere, Heminge, Condall, Philips and others, partners in the profittes of that they call the House, but makeing the leases for twenty-one yeeres hath beene the destruction of ourselves and others, for they dyeing at the expiration of three or four yeeres of their lease,[2] the

Now to a stately theatre is turned;
Which is an emblem, that great things are won
By those that dare through greatest dangers run."
John Taylor: *Quatern of new-catched Epigrams*, no. xxii., quoted by Malone, *Historical Account*, p. 70.

[1] All actors were partners in so far as the entrance fee, which was collected at the doors, was their due. But the proprietors took all that was paid for the boxes, the galleries, and the seats on the stage. For further information on this point see the following section, p. 109.

[2] All these "deserving men" were alive three or four years after the building of the Globe. The first to die was Augustine Phillips, the old clown, whose death occurred in 1605. Condell and Heminge lived respectively to 1627 and 1630. Shakespeare who, as we know, died in 1616, had probably given up his share some years previously.

6—The New Globe Theatre.

subsequent yeeres became dissolved to strangers as by marrying with their widdowes and the like by their children." [1]

In 1635 the Burbage family, though none of them acted any longer, still possessed 3½ shares of the 16, into which "The Globe" was divided; the remainder were held by the widow of Condell (2), and by the actors Robinson (3½), Schanke (3), Taylor and Lewin (each 2). [2]

While "The Globe" continued to be a sound paying business, its theatrical reputation had somewhat declined. The public which frequented it were scarcely so refined as that which went to Blackfriars, and the actors, "The King's Men," who were the same in both places, performed at "The Globe" mainly what we should call spectacular plays.

James Shirley, in the prologue of his *Rosania, or The Doubtful Heir*, gibes at his own public. His plays were to have been performed at Blackfriars, and his prologue apologises for the refined fare in these words :—

" Gentlemen, I am only sent to say,
    Our author did not calculate his play
For this meridian. The *Bankside*, he knows,
Is far more skilful at the ebbs and flows
Of water than of wit ; he did not mean
For the elevation of your poles this scene.

[1] In the reply above quoted to a complaint from some of the actors. Comp. above, p. 37.

[2] Comp. a complaint from the actors Benfield, Swanston and Pollard to the Earl of Pembroke (1635), printed in Halliwell-Phillipps's *Outlines*, pp. 539 ff.

No shews, no dance—and what you most delight in,
Grave understanders,[1] here's no target-fighting
Upon this stage ; all work for culers barr'd ;
No bawdry nor no ballads ;—this goes hard :
But language clean, and, what affects you not,
Without impossibilities the plot,
No clown, no squibs, no devil in 't.—Oh now,
You squirrels that want nuts, what will you do ?
Pray do not crack the benches, and we may
Hereafter fit your palates with a play.
But you that can contract yourselves, and fit,
As you were now in the *Blackfriars* pit,
And will not deaf us with lewd noise and tongues
Because we have no heart to break our lungs
Will pardon our *vast* stage, and not disgrace,
This play meant for your persons, not the place." [2]

These words were written and spoken in 1640. A few years later the famous " Globe" had ceased to exist. The exact date of its destruction was the 15th of April 1644, when the Puritans pulled it down.

The old home of the art of Shakespeare is now occupied by the large breweries of Barclay & Perkins.——

When in 1613 " The Globe" Theatre was entirely burned down, Henslowe at once profited by the chance offered him by the temporary incapacitation of his most dangerous competitors. He entered into partnership with the waterman, Jacob Meade, who had formerly been a

---

[1] *Grave understanders*, a very common pun on the populace in the pit, who stood below the stage. Ben Jonson also called them "the understanding gentlemen of the ground here."

[2] This prologue is printed in Malone : *Historical Account*, pp. 72 ff.

keeper of the royal animals, and immediately had his bear-circus transformed into a proper play-house, but so that it might still be used for fights between animals.

For the construction of this theatre "The Swan" was to serve as a model. We read in the contract between the carpenter and the mason on the one side, and Henslowe and Meade on the other, that in circumference and height it was to be equal to the play-house called "The Swan."

The foundation was to be of brick, and the timber in the lowest storey of oak only; the pillars likewise of oak, and turned. The stage was to be surrounded by a frame and to rest on rams, so that it might be removed when the theatre had to serve for bull-baiting and bear-baiting. The stage was to be covered by "heavens"—that is, a canopy—which was not, however, to rest on pillars on the floor; it was to be provided with leaden gutters for the rain-water to run off. The theatre was to have three storeys like "The Swan," the lowest of which was to contain some particularly comfortable boxes, "convenient and suitable for gentlemen to sit in." The roof was to be of English tiles, not thatched like the previous theatres. Finally, a tile-covered stable was to accommodate six bulls and three horses.[1]

The new play-house received the significant name of "The Hope," and the company which was engaged to act there obtained the Princess Elizabeth as patroness,

[1] The whole building contract is printed by Malone: *Variorum Shakespeare*, 343.

and called itself, after her, "The Lady Elizabeth's Servants." Its leading actor was Nathaniel Field, a young star,[1] who had already won fame as a child-actor, and who now rivalled Richard Burbage himself as the youthful hero.

Field was accompanied by a number of talented young dramatists, above all, Ben Jonson, and next to him John Fletcher, Philip Massinger, Robert Daborne, all of them tempted by old father Henslowe's gold, and all more or less in the pocket of the wily pawnbroker.

Among the papers left by Edward Alleyn are a number of letters, complaints and receipts from authors and actors who stood in business relations with Henslowe.[2] A thorough study of these old papers gives a most vivid and interesting idea of the circumstances in which dramatic authors lived at that time. It is sad and painful to see how even distinguished artists truckle and flatter in order to obtain a loan or an advance from the plebeian upstart and *nouveau riche*, as we may call Henslowe, a man who got his first start in life by marrying the wealthy woman[3] in whose service he was, —who afterwards increased his fortune by pawnbroking

[1] In 1613 he was 26 years old.

[2] These papers were published for the Shakespeare Society by J. P. Collier, partly in his *Memoirs of Alleyn*, partly in *The Alleyn Papers*, but unfortunately in a very disorderly and unchronological way. The notes and explanations, moreover, are to a great extent more misleading than instructive to anybody who is not thoroughly acquainted with the subject. Finally, these editions are marred by a number of forgeries, which are so many pitfalls for any student who has not been warned of them.

[3] From a lawsuit over Henslowe's estate after his death we are furnished with a document proving this fact, which, as far as I know, has not been noticed before : "That Philip Henslow maried Agnes at such tyme as she was his Mrs and he her servant, being wholy advanced by her . . ." *Memoirs of E. Alleyn*, p. 124.

and all kinds of more or less surreptitious theatrical enterprises, and was now a notorious usurer, scarcely able to write a single consecutive sentence, but never failing to begin his theatrical accounts with the words : " In God's name, Amen."

The actors and dramatic authors were probably, as a rule, a happy-go-lucky careless sort of folks, who were very free with their money. Celebrated and distinguished men like Field and Dekker were continually in prison arrested for debt, and obliged to turn for help to their wealthy acquaintances. Robert Daborne, a third-rate, but rather fertile author, has left a large number of notes sent to Henslowe, all without exception treating of loans and advances. We will quote one which dates from about the time when " The Hope " Theatre was opened. On August 3rd, 1613, he writes to Henslowe as follows : " Mr Hinchlow,[1] I have ever since I saw you kept my bed, being so lame that I cannot stand. I pray, S^r, goe forward with that reasonable bargain for the Bellman ;[2] we will hav but twelve pounds and the overplus of the second day, whearof I hav had ten shillings and desyre but twenty shillings more, till you have three sheets of my papers. Good S^r, consyder how for y^r sake I have put myself out of the assured way to get money, and from twenty pounds a play am come to twelv ; thearfor in my extremyty forsake me not, as y^u shall ever command me. My wife can aquaynt y^u how infinite great my occation is, and

[1] This is one of several ways in which the name of the old stage-manager is frequently spelt.

[2] *The Bellman of London*, the play at which Daborne was working at the time.

this shall be sufficient for the receipt till I come to set my hand to your book.

"Yo^r at comand,

"ROB. DABORNE.

"Aug. 3, 1613."

Below is added in Henslowe's handwriting :—

"Lent Mr Daborne upon this not the 32 of August in earnest of a playe called the Bellman of London, XXs."

Henslowe was very cunning in the way he took advantage of the difficulties of his authors and actors. He sells them costumes and ornaments on part-payment, buys plays of the authors and sells them to the actors, but keeps the manuscripts for himself. When lending money to individual actors, he charges the amount to the account of the whole company, and deducts the instalments and interests due to him from the proceeds of the performance. He never permits his companies to get entirely out of debt to him, but as soon as they are on the point of freeing themselves he stops the performances by dismissing the hired men of the company, that is, the inferior actors and functionaries with whom he had a contract, but whom he did not pay, and without whom there could be no acting. In the course of three years he dissolved five companies, for, as he said, "If those fellows come out of their debt to me, I should never have any power over them."

And indeed, the discontent with him increased more and more, and even within two years after the building of "The Hope," it broke out in a very sharply worded complaint from the actors, in which they accuse him of all the irregularities[1] we have mentioned and several others besides.

Whether the actors reaped any benefit from their complaint during Henslowe's life-time, we cannot discover, but it is not likely. However, a short time after this the old pawnbroker died (in 1616), leaving a considerable fortune (about £11,000) and an outstanding claim of £400. His son-in-law, Edward Alleyn, took on his theatrical business, and some months after the death of Henslowe,[2] made a contract with the company, according to which he released them of £200 of the debt, and allowed them to pay the remainder out of a fourth part of the proceeds of the galleries,[3] a good proof that the grievances against Henslowe were not unfounded, for Alleyn, as a rule, was close enough in money matters.

Among the names of the actors who made this contract with Alleyn we do not find that of Nathaniel Field, so at this time he must have left the company and "The Hope" Theatre, and no doubt had joined "The King's Men" (Shakespeare's old company) accompanied by Jonson, Fletcher and Massinger.

"The Globe" Theatre had risen again after the fire, and the star of "The Hope" was declining. Formerly, plays had been acted four times a week, and there had

[1] The complaint was printed by Malone from a MS. found in Dulwich College. The MS. is nowhere to be found now, but a reprint of the complaint is contained in the *Alleyn Papers*, p. 78 ff. The above characteristic utterance of Henslowe is copied literally from the complaint.

[2] Henslowe died on January 9th, 1616, and on the 20th of March in the same year Alleyn made the contract with the actors.

[3] The contract is reprinted in full in Collier's *Memoirs of E. Alleyn*, pp. 127 ff.

been bear-fights on Tuesdays and Thursdays, but
gradually the bear-fights seem to have once more gained
the upper hand; "The Hope" lost its fine name and
was commonly called the "Bear-garden,"[1] and as such it
was carried on down to 1642, when all entertainments of
the kind were forbidden.

The last news of the Bear-garden is of 1691. Then
it had become a glass factory where "crown window-
glass is made, which in all respects far exceeds French
glass."[2]

Besides the burning of "The Globe" in 1613,
London had another great conflagration at a theatre to
record during this period. In 1621 the large and
magnificent "Fortune," the first theatre in London, as it
is called by the writer of a contemporary letter,[3] was
destroyed by fire. In the course of two hours the whole
of the fine building was converted into a heap of ashes,
and the actors lost their whole wardrobe and other
equipment, as well as their expensive "play-books," that
is, the manuscripts of the plays in their repertoire.

The company which was then acting at "The
Fortune" was the same that had occupied it all along,
viz., "The Prince's Servants," originally "The Lord

---

[1] We learn this from Stow's *Survey of London*, continued by Howe, in
which we read : "The Hope on the Bankside in Southwark, commonly
called the Beare-Garden, a play-house for Stage playes on Mondayes,
Wednesdayes, Fridayes and Saturdayes ; and for the baiting of the Beares
on Tuesdayes and Thursdayes, the Stage being made to take up and down
when they plesse."

[2] Advertisement in *The Gazette* for June 18th, 1691, quoted by Ordish.

[3] John Chamberlain, in a letter of December 15th, 1621, to Sir Dudley
Carleton ; in the collection of MSS. of Dr Birch, Brit. Mus. ; discovered by
Edmond Malone (*Historical Account*, p. 55, n. 5) ; Stow's *Chronicle* (1631
edit.) also mentions the fire, but puts it down erroneously to 1617.

Admiral's Men," hitherto under the leadership of Edward Alleyn, who, however, had given up acting several years before.

If "The Fortune" is called the first theatre of the town, this must be understood to mean the most stately in appearance. As a home of dramatic art and literature it never attained the importance of "The Globe" or "The Blackfriars."

The Henslowe-Alleyn enterprises always kept a touch of a somewhat rough and business-like popularity, which certainly brought a good deal of money into the cash-box of the managers, but no corresponding artistic glory to their memory.

After the fire and the subsequent reconstruction, "The Fortune" for some years passed into the hands of another company called "The Prince Palatine's Men," which, however, was entirely dissolved in 1624, after which the old "Prince's Servants" were reinstalled under the name of "The Fortune Company," and continued acting there till the Civil War.

About the year 1630 "The Fortune" and "The Red Bull," probably used by the same company, seem to have been considered as rather cheap and common places of amusement, to judge from a passage in the introduction to *The Careless Shepherdess* by Goffe, where we read :—

　　　"I will hasten to the money-box,
　　And take my shilling out again—
　　I'll go to The Bull or Fortune, and there see
　　A play for twopence, and a jig to boot."

The last news of "The Fortune" Theatre is an

advertisement in the *Mercurius Politicus* of February 14th, 1661,[1] running thus :—

" The Fortune playhouse situate between White-cross-street and Golding-lane in the parish of Saint Giles, Cripplegate, with the ground thereto belonging, is to be lett to be built upon ; where twenty-three tenements may be erected, with gardens ; and a street may be cut through for the better accommodation of the buildings."

So in that year " The Fortune " was probably pulled down. That it could give place to twenty-three dwellings with gardens proves what a large area it must have occupied.

VIII

Number of Theatres—" The Red Bull "—The Last Theatres, " The Cockpit " or " The Phœnix" and " Salisbury Court."

WE have still to mention a few theatres of no particular importance, of the history of which very little is known.

We frequently meet with a tendency to exaggerate the number of theatres in London in the old times. Some authors mention no less than twenty-three contemporary play-houses. One of the causes of this mistake is ignorance of the fact that several theatres had double names. For instance, much has been written about a theatre called " Paris Garden," though nobody has been able to determine its dates. But " Paris Garden Theatre " is none other than " The Swan,"

[1] Discovered by Steevens and quoted by Malone, *Historical Account*, p. 55, n. 5.

which was situated on the pleasure ground south of the Thames called " Paris Garden." Thus, as we have seen above, " The Hope" was the reconstructed Bear-garden, and was still frequently called by the old name. A later theatre is called alternately " The Cockpit" and " The Phœnix," and " Salisbury Court," built in 1629, is also called " The Whitefriars." [1]

At the time when Shakespeare made his appearance in the theatrical world, about 1590, there existed in reality at most three play-houses properly so-called, " The Theatre," " The Curtain," and " Newington Butts"; and it is even doubtful whether the last-named was a real theatre. More probably it was a stage in the yard of an inn, like " The Cross Keys" and " The Red Bull," where plays were performed at the same time.

Ten years later, about 1600, " The Theatre" and " Newington" have disappeared, but five others have been added, " The Rose," " Blackfriars," " The Globe," " The Swan," and " The Fortune"—six theatres in all. Perhaps at this time " The Red Bull" was converted into a real play-house; at any rate, from about this time (1599) the Company called the " Queen's Revels" Company acted alternately on this stage and at " The Curtain."

There is not much to be said about the history of the " Red Bull." It was situated in St John's Street, Clerkenwell, probably just outside St John's Gate. In 1633 William Prynne mentions it in his *Histriomastix* as recently rebuilt and enlarged,[2] which proves its grow-

---

[1] In a marginal note to the dedicatory epistle of his *Histriomastix* (1633), "a newly-built theatre," which was " Salisbury Court," is called by William Prynne " Whitefriars' Play-house."

[2] *Histriomastix.* Epistle Dedicatory.

ing popularity. About this popularity there exists other evidence as well, but at the same time the reports speak of the low character of the amusements provided at this play-house. Thus, in a little complimentary poem written in 1630 to Davenant on the occasion of his excellent play, *The Just Italian*, Carew complains of the bad taste of the public, and of the bad and boisterous acting :—

> " Now noise prevails ; and he is taxed for drowth
>   Of wit, that with the cry spends not his mouth—
> . . . . thy strong fancies, raptures of the brain
>   Dress'd in poetick flames, they entertain
>   As a bold impious reach ; for they'll still slight
>   All that exceeds *Red Bull* and *Cockpit* flight.
>   These are the men in crowded heaps that throng
>   To that adulterate stage, where not a tongue
>   Of the untun'd kennel can a line repeat
>   Of serious sense ; but like lips meet like meat :
>   Whilst the true blood of actors, that alone
>   Keep natural unstrain'd action in their throne,
>   Behold their benches bare, though they rehearse
>   The terser Beaumont's or great Jonson's verse."

By this "true brood of actors" Carew means " The King's Men," who, as we know, were acting at the time at " The Globe " and " Blackfriars." It must be added that Davenant's play, *The Just Italian*, was performed on the latter stage.

"The Red Bull" was one of the few play-houses which survived the Civil War and the Commonwealth. Even during the protectorate of Cromwell, when all

7—Interior of the " Red Bull " Theatre.

plays were prohibited, it seems to have been used for secret performances. And after the Restoration it was the first place where the poor and miserable remains of the once proud and wealthy companies assembled under the leadership of a certain Rhodes, who was formerly a prompter at " The Blackfriars."

But these unfortunate men had a pitiful time of it. Samuel Pepys, the well-known Secretary of the Admiralty, and playgoer, whose diary is one of the principal sources for the study of the stage-history of the time of the Restoration, gives the following report of a visit he paid to the place on March 23rd, 1661 :—" To the Red Bull (where I had not been since plays come up again) up to the tireing-room, where strange confusion and disorder that there is among them in fitting themselves, especially here, where the clothes are very poore, and the actors but common fellows. At last into the pitt, where I think there was not above ten more than myself, and not one hundred in the whole house. And the play, which is called *All's Lost by Lust*, poorly done ; and with so much disorder, among others, in the musique-room, the boy that was to sing a song, not singing it right, his master fell about his ears and beat him so, that it put the whole house into an uproar."

The old theatre still existed in 1663, but at that time it must have been entirely abandoned, judging by a speech in Davenant's play, *A Theatre to Let*, where it is said to have no other lodgers than the spiders.

Afterwards, as far as I know, we hear no more about the fate of " The Red Bull."

About "The Cockpit," which we mentioned together with "The Red Bull," the information is equally scanty. As we gather from the name, it was originally a place used for cock-fights.   But as to the date at which it was rebuilt into a real theatre, there is no more accurate information than a passage in *Camden's* "Annals of James I.," in 1617, where he speaks of it as newly erected (*nuper erectum*).[1]

In Stow's *Chronicle* of the same year it is spoken of as "a new play-house."

In this year, on Shrove Tuesday, it was stormed and pillaged by London apprentices, who set fire to it, so that it was burned down.   Neither "The Cockpit" nor Drury Lane, the quarter in which it was situated, bore a good reputation.   It was not uncommon, on the whole, for a number of public-houses of more or less bad repute, to gather round the theatres, and here the disorderly element in the pit-audience sought refuge after the performance.   And such ill-famed houses the apprentices of the time considered it their privilege to attack during Shrovetide, when they had their liberty and were allowed to kick over the traces.

Whether they fell on the theatre by mistake instead of on the neighbouring houses of ill-fame, or whether "The Cockpit" Theatre was really so disorderly that it deserved no better name than the one which the stage-manager in Zola's "Nana" gives to his own theatre, we are unable to tell.

If we are to believe the old enemy of theatres, the Puritan Prynne, the play-houses of his time were not

[1] Comp. Collier: *History of English Dramatic Poetry*, iii. 136.

much better than their improper neighbours. In a passage in his extensive work " Histriomastix," he first tells us how the theatres of the Greeks and Romans were the homes of unchastity, and that there young women were simply trained for houses of ill-fame. " How farre this usage yet continues I cannot positively determine; yet this I have heard by good intelligence that our common Strumpets and Adulteresses after our Stage-plays ended, are oft-times prostituted neere our Play-houses, if not in them; that our Theaters if they are not Bawdy-houses (as they may easily be, since many Players, if reports be true, are common Panders) yet they are Cosin-germanes, at leastwise neighbours to them: Witnesse the Cockpit and Drury-lane; Black-friers Playhouse, and Duke-Humfries; the Red-bull, and Turnbull-street; the Globe, and Bank-side Brothel-houses." [1]

Though certainly we cannot attach much credit to good Mr Prynne, who, like so many other pretended " saints," had the foible of indulging too much in gossip upon sensual matters, there can scarcely be any doubt that " The Cockpit" neither was nor ever became a theatre of good reputation. Probably after its destruction in 1617 it adopted the name of " The Phœnix," but generally we find it called by its original name. Nor did the old " Bear-garden" succeed in persuading the public to adopt the finer name of " The Hope," which was given it by Henslowe in 1614.

In " The Cockpit" or " The Phœnix," the per-

[1] W. Prynne: *Histriomastix, or the Players Scourge*, 1633, pp. 390 f.

formances were mainly given by "The Queen's Men," afterwards called "Beeston's Boys." It continued to exist after the Restoration, but it lost all importance when in the year 1663 the new Drury Lane Theatre, called "The Theatre Royal, Drury Lane,"—which was not situated on the same site as "The Cockpit"—was opened by Sir William Davenant.

There is still one little theatre—the last built during this period—of which we have a few words to say.

We have mentioned above that "The Whitefriars" and "The Salisbury Court" Theatre were one and the same. This, however, means that "The Salisbury Court," which was built in 1629 close to the old Whitefriars' monastery or on its site, was now and then mentioned by the old monastic name, like "The Blackfriars" Theatre, though the latter had no other name.

The old Whitefriars monastery of which Shakespeare speaks in his *Richard III*.[1] no longer existed as such in his time. It had given place to a number of splendid dwellings for noblemen and other rich people. But the old dilapidated refectory was used now and then—probably not often—for dramatic performances. I am inclined to believe that when, in 1608, "The King's Servant's" drove "The Queen's Children" away from Blackfriars,[2] the latter went to the old refectory of Whitefriars and tried their fortune there. At any rate,

[1] *Gloster.* Take up the corse, Sirs.
  Gentleman. Towards Chertsey, noble lord?
  Gloster. No, to Whitefriars ; there attend my coming.
                                        Richard III. i. 2.
[2] See above, p. 38.

Nathaniel Field, the principal actor among "The Queen's Children," acted his play *A Woman is a Weather-cock* here about, or rather before, 1610. And before this period we hear nothing about performances at "The Whitefriars."

It is not likely that this monastic hall was ever converted into a real theatre. When "Salisbury Court" was built, it was on another site, though in the immediate vicinity, and, no doubt, it was quite a new building. The English conservatism, which in this case is highly praiseworthy, and owing to which the names of the streets in London are like a hand-book of the history of the town, has also preserved the names of these two old theatres in the two streets, Whitefriars Street and Salisbury Court. They are situated in the central and the busiest part of the town, both running into Fleet Street.

We can say, then, in a certain sense that there was a "Whitefriars' Theatre," the old hall of the monastery, which was now and then used for dramatic performances, and the more recent "Salisbury Court," which was a real theatre, and which, we may be sure, rendered the monastic hall quite superfluous, so that they did not exist contemporaneously.

The new theatre seems to have been successful, but not immediately. There is reason to believe that it was first hired by a company which at that time bore the name of "The Children of the King's Revels."[1] This

---

[1] The same which had formerly been called "The Queen's Children," but which after the death of Queen Anne, the wife of James I., received the above name.

was scarcely a very distinguished company; still, in 1632, it had plays written for its performances by so noted an author as Shirley. In the same year " The King's Children "—not to be confounded with " The King's Servants," Shakespeare's old company—had to leave " Salisbury Court " and go to the less-esteemed " Fortune," while " Prince Charles's Men " moved into the new little theatre, and immediately had a success in *Holland's Leaguer*, the first amusing play by Marmyon. Richard Brome also wrote for " Salisbury Court," where his *Antipodes* was acted in 1638 by " The Queen's Men."

On the whole the little theatre, about the exterior or interior of which we know nothing except that, like " The Cockpit," it was a private—which means a closed-in and roofed—theatre, enjoyed a good reputation, and may be ranked next to " The Blackfriars " and " The Globe."

It survived the time of the Commonwealth, and was used for acting after the Restoration, but was then called " The Theatre in Dorset Court."

A general survey of the London Theatres between 1576 and 1642.

" THE THEATRE."	Built, 1576; pulled down, 1598; proprietor, Burbage; company, the Lord Chamberlain's; situation, Shoreditch, north-east of London; public theatre.
" THE CURTAIN."	Built, 1576 or 1577; date of destruction, unknown; proprietor, unknown; company, the Lord Chamberlain's, afterwards the Queen's and the Prince's; situation, Shoreditch; public theatre.

"NEWINGTON BUTTS."	Dates of building and destruction, unknown; proprietor, Henslowe; company, the Lord Admiral's; situation, Newington (Lambeth), south side of London, right bank of the Thames; public theatre (?).
"THE ROSE."	Built, 1592; date of destruction, unknown; proprietor, Henslowe; company, the Lord Admiral's; situation, Bankside, southern bank of the Thames; public theatre.
"BLACKFRIARS."	Built, 1596; pulled down, 1647 (?); proprietor, J. Burbage and heirs; company, the Chapel Children—after 1608, the King's; situation, present Queen Victoria Street, City; private theatre.
"THE SWAN" OR "PARIS GARDEN."	Built, about 1596 (?); date of destruction, unknown; proprietor, Francis Langley; company, unknown; situation, Paris Garden, Bankside; public theatre.
"GLOBE."	Built, 1598; burned, 1613; rebuilt, 1614; pulled down, 1644; proprietors, Richard and Cuthbert Burbage; company, the King's; situation, Bankside, near St Saviour's; public theatre.
"FORTUNE."	Built, 1599; burned, 1621; rebuilt, 1622 (?); pulled down, about 1661; proprietors, Henslowe and Alleyn; company, the Lord Admiral's (the Prince's, the Fortune's); situation, Golden Lane, Middlesex; public theatre.
"RED BULL."	Built, about 1599 (?); rebuilt, about 1630 (?); pulled down, about 1663 (?); proprietor, unknown; company, the Queen's (the Prince's, Bull Company); situation, St John Street, Clerkenwell; private theatre.
"HOPE" OR "BEAR-GARDEN."	Built (as theatre), 1613; pulled down, about 1644 (?); proprietors, Henslowe and Alleyn; company, the Lady Elizabeth's; situation, Bankside; public theatre.

" COCKPIT " OR " PHŒNIX."	Built, about 1615 (?); pulled down, after 1663 ; proprietor, unknown ; company, the Lady Elizabeth's (the Queen's, Beeston's Boys); situation, Drury Lane; private theatre.
" SALISBURY COURT " OR " WHITEFRIARS."	Built, 1629 ; pulled down (?), after the Restoration ; proprietor, unknown; company, Children of the Revels and the Prince's; situation, Salisbury Court (close to Fleet Street) ; private theatre.

GENERAL THEATRICAL CONDITIONS

I

Hours of Performance—Play-bills—Taylor's Rhyming Matches—Prices of
Admission and Gatherers—Proceeds of the Performances, and Fees
Paid by the Court—Accommodation.

WHEN the trumpets sent out their shrill blasts over the
roofs of London, and coloured silk flags were hoisted on
the masts of the little garret-like towers which rose from
the top of the circular walls enclosing the theatres, when
the multifarious signs, the Swan, Atlas carrying the globe,
the Goddess of Fortune, and the rest, were swinging in
the wind, everybody knew that the theatrical performances
were going to begin, and playgoers made haste to finish
their dinner in order to secure a good seat in time.

In the earliest times, when the taste for theatrical
entertainments was reaching its height, though the
number of play-houses was small, people frequently
neglected their dinner and took their seats a long time
in advance, waiting patiently for the beginning of the
play; if they caught sight of an actor peeping out from
behind the draperies in the background to watch the
filling of the house, they would greet him respectfully.[1]

It was the custom to attend to business early in the

---

[1] " For they to theatres were pleased to come,
  Ere they had din'd, to take up the best room ;
  There sat on benches not adorn'd with mats,
  And graciously did veil their high-crown'd hats

day; eleven o'clock was the hour for the Exchange, and twelve was dinner-time. So the play probably commenced between one and two. But this was in the good old times at the close of the sixteenth century; we soon hear of the "modern" fashion of dining as late as two o'clock,[1] and the theatre, which has always very much depended on people's dinner-time, had to put off the play till three o'clock.

On particular occasions, for instance, when a new play was to be performed, it became the custom to secure a place in time by sending a servant who occupied a seat till his master arrived. On the whole, it was considered more distinguished to create a little sensation by delaying one's entrance till after the beginning of the performance.

During the earliest period of the theatres there were performances every day, including Sundays, though not during the hours of service, and this fashion continued during the time of Queen Elizabeth, to the great annoyance of the Puritans, who had to endure the reconciliation by the head of the empire of the duties as Christian Majesty with her presence at dramatic performances on holidays. A prohibition from the Lord Mayor in 1580 was not obeyed. Under James I. public performances on Sundays were indeed forbidden by an Act of Parliament, but the Court did not comply with this order, and King James found pleasure in going to plays and masques,

> To every half-dress'd player, as he still
> Through hangings peep'd to see the galleries fill."
>   Davenant : Prologue to *The Unfortunate Lovers*, quoted
>   by Malone, *Historical Account*, p. 157, n. 9.
> [1] Dekker : *The Gull's Horn-book*, 1609.

of which he was very fond, on Sundays as well as on week days.

Though no daily press existed in the time of Shakespeare, the public had no great difficulty in learning which plays were to be acted in the theatres.

The "water-poet," Taylor, in one of his humorous writings,[1] tells us a little "quiblet" about Field, which shows this very clearly: "Master Field, the player, riding up Fleet Street a great pace, a gentleman called to him, and asked him what play was played that day? He (being angry to be stayed on so frivolous a demand) answered that he might see what play was to be played upon every *post*. I cry you mercy (said the gentleman); I took you for a *post*, you rode so fast."

So this was the custom. Printed bills were stuck on posts [2]—just as they are now—on which the title of the play was announced, but neither the name of the author nor those of the actors. In another place the same "water-poet" also informs us of the number of bills that were usually printed.

Once—it was in 1614—he had challenged the rhymer, William Fennor, to a competition in the art of improvised rhyming. The match was to take place in "The Hope" Theatre, but the false rhymer Fennor left the water-poet in the lurch, and kept away on the day of performance. The affair created some sensation, and

---

[1] John Taylor: *Wit and Mirth*; the anecdote is called "a quiblet."

[2] "They use to set up their billes upon posts some certaine days before, to admonish the people to make resort to their theatres, that they may thereby be the better furnished and the people prepared to fill their purses with their treasures."—John Northbrook: *Treatise against Idleness, vaine Playes and Interludes*.

Taylor wrote an indignant pamphlet in verse about the disgraceful way in which he had been treated. He says in the Preface: " Bee it therefore knowne unto all men that I, John Taylor, Waterman, did agree with William Fennor (who arrogantly and falsely entitles himselfe the King's Majesties Riming Poet) to answer me at a triall of Wit, on the seventh of October last 1614 on the Hope Stage on the Bankside, and the said Fennor received of mee ten shillings in earnest of his comming to meet me, whereupon I caused 1000 bills to be Printed, and divulg'd my name 1000 wayes and more, giving my Friends and divers of my acquaintance notice of this Bear Garden banquet of dainty conceits; and when the day came that the Play should have been performed, the hous being fill'd with a great Audience, who had all spent their monies extraordinarily: then this Companion for an Asse, ran away and left me for a Foole, amongst thousands of critical Censurers, when I was ill thought of by my friends, scorned by my foes and in conclusion in a greater puzzell than the blinde Beare in the midst of all her whipbroth; Besides the summe of twenty pounds in money I lost my reputation amongst many and gained disgrace instead of my better expectations."

From this we see that a thousand printed bills were put up, at all events on special occasions; for ordinary performances this number seems disproportionately large.[1]

Strange to say, as far as I know, none of the printed play-bills of the time have been preserved or discovered. But among the many treasures [2] of Dulwich College we

[1] *Taylor's Revenge, or the Rimer William Fennor firkt, ferrited, and finely fetcht over the coales.*—Taylor's *Works*, 1630, pp. 142 ff.

[2] Warne's *Catalogue*, etc., p. 83 (Ordish, 236).

have discovered a hand-written bill of a bear-fight, probably the MS. of the printed one. It dates from the time of James I., and as the only authentic memorial of the theatrical advertisements of the period, it may find a place here. It runs as follows :—

"Tomorrowe beinge Thursdaie shalbe seen at the Beargarden on the banckside a greate mach plaid by the gamsters of Essex, who hath chalenged all comers whatsoever to plaie V dogges at the single beare for V pounds, and also to wearie a bull dead at the stake ; and for your better content shall have plasant sport with the horse and ape and wiping of the blind beare. Vivat Rex !"

We may, however, to a certain extent draw our own conclusions as to the form of the playbills by reading the "long-tailed" titles [1] which were given to books by the printers, *e.g.* in the earliest quarto editions of some of Shakespeare's dramas. A few examples will show the style. *Henry IV.* receives the following title : "The History of Henrie the Fourth ; With the battell at Shrewsburie, between the King and Lord Henry Percy, surnamed Henrie Hotspur of the North. With the humorous conceits of Sir John Falstalffe."

The Merchant of Venice starts with a still longer recommendation : "The Excellent History of the Merchant of Venice. With the extreme cruelty of Shylocke the Jew towards the said Merchant, in cutting a just pound of his flesh. And the obtaining of Portia, by the choyse of three Caskets."

This is how *King Lear* makes his appearance :

---

[1] This expression is used by Thomas Nash in the Preface of his play, *Pierce Penniless*. He writes to his printer : "First of all cut off the long-tailed title."

" Mr William Shakespeare, His True Chronicle History of the life and death of King Lear, and his three Daughters. With the unfortunate life of Edgar, sonne and heir to the Earle of Glocester, and his sullen and assumed humour of Tom of Bedlam. As it was plaid before the King's Majesty at White-Hall, upon S. Stephens night, in Christmas Hollidaies." [1]

The playbills do not give the names of the persons represented or of the actors. The custom of doing so was probably not introduced into England before the eighteenth century. [2]

In *A Midsummer Night's Dream* Shakespeare himself makes fun of the ludicrous playbills by making Philostrate read out about: "a tedious brief scene of young Pyramus, And his love Thisbe; very tragical mirth."

The prices of admission were not written on the playbills, but several passages in the dramatic literature

[1] These circumstantial programmes went to Germany with the travelling English companies, and in that country grew to a unique degree of tasteless length. In a Gotha play-calendar of 1783 I find the following magnificently florid play-bill of Hamlet : " Indeed Landshut never saw a grander play !— What thoughts ! Exalted, stirring, incomparable ! One Shakespear [*sic*] has existed in the world, who has written in such a masterly way and rendered himself immortal in both posterities [!] There is but one Hamlet who can make the spectator's blood run cold, oppress his heart and make his senses feel eternity. This tragedy is a true and horrible story from Denmark, and in a way which makes us shiver it contains the law of retribution." (Then follows an account of the subject. In its German form the play ends with these words : " Hamlet mounts on his lawful throne " . . .). "Where could there be a man who would not like to see and admire Hamlet and pay his respects to him and tender him his applause." After this we cannot wonder at the German title given to another Shakespearean tragedy, *Richard III.* : " Richard der dritte, oder der grausame Protektor " ; or that a seventeenth century adaptation of Hamlet bears the title : " Der bestrafte Brudermord oder Prinz Hamlet aus Dänemark."

[2] J. P. Collier, indeed, presents us with a playbill of 1663, containing a complete list of the players and the characters represented, but this document must undoubtedly be regarded with great suspicion.

of the time enable us to form an idea of the usual entrance fee, though not of the exact prices of the different places in each theatre ; nor would this be of any particular interest.

As far as we can judge from illustrations, the theatres of the Shakespearean period had only one entrance, probably for the practical purpose of simplifying the collection of the fees and rendering it difficult for the public to slip into the theatre without paying.

At the entrance stood the trusted man of the company, the "gatherer," with his cash-box, in which he collected the sixpences, which he afterwards delivered to the leading actor. Inside the theatre were several gatherers, who claimed the extra prices for the better seats. These gatherers were sometimes women. To the inferior actors it was a coveted addition to their income to have their wives employed as gatherers.[1] It is, as far as I know, the only employment a woman could obtain at the old English theatres. We are aware that no woman appeared on the stage either as an actress or as a super.

Among the Alleyn Papers there is a short letter from the actor, William Birde, in which he speaks of the gatherer's functions, and which, we suppose, is the only direct testimony about these functionaries. As it affords us a good peep behind the scenes, and as it is very little known, I do not hesitate to quote it here. It runs as follows :—

"SIR,

"There is one John Russell, that by your appoynt-

---

[1] Comp. *Alleyn Papers*, p. 51, where the wife of the actor Rose is recommended for such a post.

ment was made a gatherer with us, but my fellowes finding [him often] falce to us, have many tymes warnd him from taking the box ; and he as often, with moste damnable othes, hath vowde never to touch ; yet, notwithstanding his excecrable othes, he hath taken the box, and many tymes moste unconscionablye gathered, for which we have resolved he shall never more come to the doore.   Yet, for your sake, he shall have his wages, to be a necessary atendaunt on the stage,[1] and if he will pleasure himself and us to mend our garments, when he hath leysure, weele pay him for that to.   I pray send us word if this motion will satisfye you ; for him, his dishonestye is such we knowe it will not.

" Thus yealding ourselves in that and a farr greater matter to be comanded by you, I commit you to God.

" Your loving friend to commaund,

" W. Birde.

" To his loving frend, Mr Allin, give these."[2]

With regard to one of the theatres we happen to possess minute information about the scale of admission fees. *Bartholomew Fair*, a comedy by Ben Jonson, which was played at " The Hope " in 1614, has an induction acted by various functionaries—the stage-keeper, the book-holder, and the scrivener, in which Jonson writes very sarcastically of the audience.   He makes a sort of bargain with the spectators, and says,

[1] It has been mentioned above, p. 6, that the gatherers also served as supers.

[2] The last line is the usual form of address on the letters of those times. The MS. of the above was in the possession of Halliwell-Phillipps, the Shakespeare expert.   It is printed in Collier's *Alleyn Papers*, pp. 32 f.

among other things : " It is further agreed that every
person here have his or their free-will of censure, to like
or dislike at their own charge, the author having now
departed with his right ; it shall be lawful for any man
to judge his six-pen' worth, his twelve-pen' worth, so to
his eighteen-pence, two shillings, half-a-crown, to the
value of his place ; provided always his place get not
above his wit. And if he pay for half-a-dozen, he may
censure for all them too, so that he will undertake that
they shall be silent. He shall put in for censures here
as they do for lots at the lottery ; marry, if he drops
but sixpence at the door, and will censure a crown's
worth, it is thought there is no conscience or justice in
that." [1]

From this we gather that the cheapest place cost
sixpence, the dearest half-a-crown. Other passages in
contemporary plays and pamphlets confirm Ben Jonson's
statement ; others again speak of lower prices, even down
to 1d. However, we have no particular reason to stop
and consider the apparent divergency in the reports
about the admission fees. Of course, they were not
quite stationary in those times, any more than they are
now, nor were they the same in the various theatres.
Thus we know that the prices were doubled, nay, sometimes trebled, at the first performances,[2] and, very likely,

[1] Ben Jonson : *Bartholomew Fair*.
[2] Scarcely, however, in the proper Shakespearean time. In the prologue
of a play of 1678 we read the following lines :—
  " An actress in a cloud's a strange surprise,
    And you ne'er paid treble prices to be wise."
There are many testimonies to prove that even in early times the prices
were raised when anything particular was played.

the prices were lowered in bad times, or when the plays were performed by inferior companies.

There is no reason to think, for instance, that " The Earl of Sussex's Men " could obtain the same prices as " The Lord Chamberlain's Company," even if they acted in the same theatre.

However, in the main, we may safely assume that the scale of prices mentioned by Ben Jonson was the normal one for good companies, and, on the whole, was maintained without much alteration from the earliest days of the theatres down to the Civil War in 1642.

So the prices were by no means low, if we consider that the corresponding value in our own days would make at least eight times the amount.

Twenty pounds seems to have been a good average result from one performance in a well-filled theatre. It was, as we see, the sum which John Taylor lost by his failure in the " Hope," and it was the amount paid by the Queen to a company when she ordered it to perform at court in the usual hours of performance in the theatre.

Royal persons, it must be observed, did not go to the theatres, but the actors were engaged to play at the palaces, and received a salary for it. As a rule the performances at court took place in the evening, so that they did not collide with the public performances. In these cases only £10 was paid, which thus gave a net profit. But if a company was ordered to play at the usual hours of performance in the theatre they received £20, in order to cover the remuneration which they lost.

If we fix the average price of admission at a shilling, we get the result that a well-filled house did not hold more than about 400 persons, a number which surprises us by its smallness, and which, indeed, differs widely from the above-quoted statement by de Witt that "The Swan" Theatre was able to hold 3000 persons. Nevertheless, it seems to me nearer the truth than the latter number. For, as a matter of fact, the theatres were all comparatively small, and the stage, which protruded far out, took up a great part of the pit, whereas a theatre which is to hold 3000 persons must be of colossal dimensions, especially if there are only three galleries, and a fourth part of the floor is occupied by the stage.

We may no doubt safely assume that no theatre of the Shakespearean period was able to hold more than 600 persons.

II

Expenses Then and Now—The Stage and its Equipment—Spectators on the Stage.

THOUGH, as we have seen, the English theatres of those times were not able to hold very large crowds of people, they were, on the whole, very profitable enterprises. This was due to the smallness of the expense connected with them. From many of the expenses, which now weigh heavily in the manager's budget, and at any rate make the working of a theatre a very risky enterprise, the theatres of those times were entirely or partly exempt. We need only think of such an item as the lighting of the house, of which most theatres, where the acting took place by daylight and in the open air, knew nothing, and which even in the closed theatres amounted to a very small sum compared with the weight of this burden nowadays.

We need say nothing of the large and complicated system of scenery and mechanism, which is the worst impediment to modern dramatic art, exceedingly expensive, as it always is, but usually without any power of creating illusion, and very frequently ugly and devoid of style. With such impediments the old English actors and managers were not troubled, and much time and money were thus saved.

We must not fancy, however, that in those times expensive scenic equipment was quite unknown in England. At court festivals enormous sums were spent on decorations imported from Italy and France, under the auspices of Inigo Jones, the collaborator and afterwards the bitter enemy[1] of Ben Jonson. But the stage-managers justly reasoned that a public which paid sixpence or a shilling to see a play could not expect thousands of pounds to be spent on an equipment, which would perhaps be useless after a few performances. And thereby they wisely saved a good deal of money.

They saved also a great deal of time. Probably no outsider has any idea what a disproportionate amount of time, trouble and worry is lavished on modern scenic equipment, with a result which in most cases lacks artistic refinement and style. Several months' toil is

[1] The enmity between Inigo Jones and Ben Jonson partly dated from the time when Jones claimed to have his name put first on the title-page as author of the "Masques" of Ben Jonson, which he had equipped, and for which he had arranged the machinery. Ben Jonson was blamed for having called Inigo Jones a fool. "I never said so," Jonson positively declared, "but I have said that he is an arch scoundrel, and this I maintain." (*Ben Jonson's Conversations with Drummond*, Lond. 1842, p. 31.)

frequently spent on plays which are not performed more than a few times. But even if justice is done to the scenery, and the expenses are covered by the number of times the play is acted, much time is lost in other ways by the present method of equipment.

A great Shakespearean drama performed in modern style with many changes of scene, in which all the workmen in the theatre, painters, joiners, smiths, upholsterers and scene-shifters, have done their best to render the scenery as illusive as possible, could not possibly be acted in its original form within a reasonable space of time. The old pieces have to be cut down, and the process has to be conducted so thoroughly that much which is good and important is necessarily lost.[1] In Shakespeare's time his own plays and those of his companions were acted all through and without omissions during two or three hours — the general duration in those times of what we call a full-length play. Fortunately the public of the time was able to enjoy fine and witty speeches well delivered, without demanding that the actors should be picturesque accessories to the scenes produced by the scene-shifters and scene-painters.

[1] On the whole, I see no sacrilege in omitting passages of the works of Shakespeare and other classics. Let us recall Ben Jonson's words : " I remember, the players have often mentioned it as an honour to Shakespeare, that in his writing, whatsoe'er he penned, he never blotted out a line. My answer hath beene, would he had blotted a thousand ;—which they thought a malevolent speech. I had not told posterity this, but for their ignorance, who choose that circumstance to commend their friend by wherein he most faulted ; and to justify my own candour,—for I lov'd the man, and doe honour his memory, on this side idolatry, as much as any." Ben Jonson's *Timber or Discoveries*, 1641, reprinted by Halliwell-Phillipps, *Outlines*, p. 649. Those who cannot see spots in Shakespeare may easily be suspected of being equally unable to measure the highest summits of art to which this marvellous poet ascended.

I have given elsewhere [1] a connected account of the development of the stage from the Middle Ages to the Renaissance, and I have shown that the English stage did not materially differ from the simple stage-platforms of the rest of Europe, though there were several peculiarities in the auditorium and the outward shape of the theatre.   I consider it superfluous to repeat in detail what has been described already.

Indeed, there is nothing obscure in the arrangement of the old English stage.   The many confused and erroneous statements which, in spite of this, we find even in the most recent works on Shakespeare, are probably due to the fact that the principal stress in these works is generally laid on the critical appreciation of the dramatic literature of the period, while the archæological side is neglected, so that one writer copies from another the theories which were current fifty or a hundred years ago, without investigating the later incidental discoveries of pictures and documents which have now given us a full and clear idea of the Shakespearean stage.

We do not think it unreasonable, however, to drive a stake through the heart of the constantly recurring delusion about a front curtain of that stage, and of that also about the fantastic borders representing "heaven" or the blue air, which are still haunting the imagination of more than one student and casting a shadow over their idea about the stage.

The stage of Shakespeare had no front curtain, and could not have had one.

It was a platform projecting into the audience and open on three sides.   If it had been covered before the

[1] In vol. ii. of the present work.

beginning of the performance or between the acts, there must have been three curtains, which, like other curtains, must have been suspended on something. That would have necessitated poles or columns at the corners of the stage, between which the curtains might be pulled. But of all this there is no vestige on the Renaissance stage whether in England or elsewhere.

But the Shakespearean theatre, like all other European stage-platforms, had a back curtain, that is, a drapery which separated the stage properly so-called from the tiring-house. How this drapery was used, and how the room behind it was sometimes added to the scene of action, are matters of which I have given a detailed account in the above-mentioned passage of vol. ii. of the present work.[1]

A glance at the three drawings of stages, figs. 3 and 7, and at the illustration discovered by Gaedertz, will give a very clear idea of the state of things. The small drawing from the title-page of Alabaster's " Roxana " is especially instructive.

This illustration, which as yet is not widely known, shows us also that the stage was sometimes surrounded by a low railing on the three sides which turned towards the public, probably in order to serve as protection against the too indiscreet approaches of the audience.[2]

[1] *Middle Ages and Renaissance*, pp. 317-323.

[2] That in some theatres these balustrades surrounded the stage is shown also by the two following quotations :—

> " And now that I have vaulted up so hye,
> Above the *stage-rayles* of this earthen globe,
> I must turn actor."   (*Black Booke*, 1604).

> " Monsieur, you may draw up your troop of force
> Within *the pales*."
>   (Davenant's *The Play-house to be let*.
>   Quoted by Malone, *Historical Account*, p. 123, n. 3.)

As to the so-called " heavens," such objects really
existed, but they had certainly as little resemblance to
our modern top-borders as a tester made by an up-
holsterer has to " this most excellent canopy, the air."
The " heavens" were a kind of awning fastened to the
tiring-house, and protecting part of the stage against
rain, for which purpose they were provided with leaden
gutters.   In this way, as we have seen, they were
arranged in " The Fortune " theatre (comp. above, p. 67).
Of course it is entirely out of the question that there
should have been any kind of decoration corresponding
to our borders on this stage-platform, which was quite
open and undecorated ; and the space behind it, which
was roofed, generally represented a room, and, therefore,
could not have wanted such decoration.

We see, then, that scarcely any money was spent in
the equipment of the stage, except on the properties
which were needed in the plays, but which can hardly be
called stage furniture.   And even these were neither very
numerous nor very expensive.   We have an inventory of
Henslowe's of March 10th, 1598,[1] containing a list of all
the properties of " The Lord Admiral's Men," which
contained altogether only thirty-five items.   Some of
these are very curious and give an insight into the
theatrical life of the time.   I quote a few of them :—

Item, I Rock, I Bow, I Grave, I Mouth of Hell.[1]

Item, II Marchpanes [artificial loaves] and the City
of Rome.

---

[1] Published by Malone, *Historical Account* (additions), pp. 377 ff., and
after him by Collier in *English Dramatic Poetry*, iii. pp. 158 ff.   The MS.
is now lost.

Item, I Lionshide, I Bearshide, and Faeton's limbs, and Faeton's ear, and Argosses [*i.e.* Argus's] head.

Item, Ierosses [*i.e.* Iris's] Head and Rainbow, I little Alter.

Item, Cupedes Bow and quiver, the Cloth with Sun and Moon.[2]

Item, A Boar's Head and Serberosses [*i.e.* Cerberus's] III Heads.

Item, Mercury's Wings, Tasso Picture, I Helmet with a Dragon, I Shield with III Lions, a Shovel of elmwood.

Item, III Tamburines, I Dragon in Faustes [Dr Faustus].

Item, III Imperial Crowns, I plain Crown.

Item, I Ghost's Crown, I Crown with a Sun.

Item, I Kettle for the Jew [*i.e. The Jew of Malta* by Marlowe].

The scenic equipment, therefore, was anything but expensive, and the theatre derived even more profit from the stage than it does at present.

From the beginning of the seventeenth century—scarcely before, or, at all events, there is nothing to prove it—places were hired for money on the stage itself. At the outset nicely furnished boxes were let to distinguished gentlemen in the galleries opposite to the stage (comp. fig. 3); but it soon became fashionable for

---

[1] From mediæval times onwards the entrance into hell had been represented by a dragon's mouth.

[2] This little cloth, the object of which we do not know, has caused the belief that painted scenery was used.

young gallants and gulls to place themselves on the very stage, where they entered deliberately from behind the back curtain, and seated themselves on small three-legged stools, which were let for this purpose by the actors for an extra payment of a shilling or sixpence.

Thomas Dekker in his "Gull's Hornbook" (1609) has a chapter which he calls "How a gallant is to behave himself in a theatre,"[1] in which he gives an amusing and graphic description of the conceited way in which young dandies exhibited themselves on the stage. He writes :—

" Present not your selfe on the stage (especially at a new play) until the quaking prologue is ready to enter ; for then it is time, as though you were one of the properties, or that you dropt of [*i.e.* off] the hangings, to creep from behind the arras, with your tripos or *three-legged stoole* in one hand, and a *teston*[2] mounted between a fore-finger and a thumb, in the other ; for if you should bestow your person upon the vulgar, when the belly of the house is but half full, your apparel is quite eaten up, the fashion lost, and the proportion of your body in more danger to be devoured, than if it were served up in the counter amongst the poultry.[3]   Avoid this as you would the baston."

It was still more fashionable to be attended by a page, who stood behind the stool on which his master

---

[1] Quoted in Malone : *Historical Account*, p. 80, n. 4.
[2] A silver coin worth sixpence.
[3] In Shakespeare's time there was a prison in London called the Poultry Compter, in which the prisoners were fed with remnants from the sheriff's table.

was seated smoking his pipe.[1] When the pipe was empty, and his master handed it to him with a lazy gesture, it was his duty to refill and relight it.

This bad custom of providing seats for spectators on the stage itself became more and more prevalent; it was done partly in order to increase the proceeds, partly to satisfy the vain desire of the many dandies to display themselves before the public. As late as the beginning of the seventeenth century this custom does not seem to have been quite common, nor generally allowed. In the Induction of John Marston's "Malcontent" (printed in 1604, performed without the Induction in 1601 at Black-friars) we find a little scene which enables us to draw this conclusion. In this Induction—which is of some interest in theatrical history—the comic actor William Sly personates such a young dandy who wants to force himself on to the stage, and the following dialogue takes place between him and the tireman, who follows him with a stool in his hand :—

Tireman. Sir, the gentlemen [2] will be angry if you sit here.

[1] " When young Rogero goes to see a play
His pleasure is you place him on the stage,
The better to demonstrate his array,
And how he sits attended by his page."

H. Parrot : *Laquei Ridiculosi,* or *Springes for Woodcocks,* 1613.

" The Globe to-morrow acts a pleasant play ;
In hearing it consume the irksome day ;
Go, take a pipe of To : the crowded stage
Must needs be greced with you and your page."

Henry Hutton : *Folly's Anatomy,* 1619, quoted by Malone, *Historical Account,* p. 82.

[2] The actors had a right to call themselves gentlemen.

Sly. Why; we may sit upon the stage at a *private* house. Thou dost not take me for a country gentleman, dost? Dost thou think I fear hissing? I'll hold my life thou tookest me for one of the players.

Tireman. No, sir.

Sly. By God's slid,[1] if you had, I would have given you but sixpence for your stool.

The spectators who wanted places on the stage did not pass through the ordinary entrance, but through the tiring-house, and here they paid the regular fee, while the sixpence or shilling for the stool was extra. And this tiring-house due was soon relied upon[2] as a fixed income.

But this custom, though it might considerably increase the daily proceeds, soon became an intolerable nuisance to the actors, who were annoyed and disturbed in their performance by the number of restless gallants. The latter, however, were not easily driven away from their time-honoured places, and in the end a royal proclamation was required to restore order on the stage. In February 1665 an order was issued in which we read: "Whereas complaint hath been made unto us of great disorders in the Attiring-house of the Theatre of our dearest brother the Duke of York, under the government of our trusty and well beloved Sir Wm. Davenant, by the resort of persons thither, to the hinderance of the actors and interruption of the scenes. Our will and

[1] Senseless oaths of this kind were fashionable among the gallants, and the plays of the time frequently mock this bad habit. Compare, for instance, Ben Jonson's *Every Man in His Humour.*

[2] This appears distinctly from an actor's contract of 1614, in which these tiring-house dues are mentioned several times. Comp. the *Alleyn Papers,* p. 76.

pleasure is, that no person of what quality soever do presume to enter at the door of the Attiring-house, but such only as do belong to the Company, and are employed by them. Requiring the guards attending there and all whom it may concern to see that obedience be given hereunto." [1]

III

Authors' fees—Censorship—Sir Henry Herbert's notes—Shakespeare's fame
   as an author.

ANOTHER thing which rendered the position of manager so profitable was the comparatively small fees paid for the pieces.

Unfortunately we have no means of ascertaining how much Shakespeare received for his plays. He wrote exclusively for one particular company — " The Lord Chamberlain's," afterwards " The King's Men " — and from this company nothing in the way of accounts has ever come to light. But with regard to the money matters of other authors, Henslowe's *Diary* and the *Alleyn Papers* afford much valuable information.

---

[1] Printed by Collier from a manuscript in the State Paper Office, *English Dramatic Poetry*, iii. p. 154, n. 2. In France the same bad habit flourished at the time of Molière. Chappuzeau writes (1674) in his *Théâtre Français* (livre iii. p. 153): " Les Acteurs ont souvent de la peine à se ranger sur le Théâtre, tant les ailes sont remplies de gens de qualité qui n'en peuvent faire qu'un riche ornement." The French stage, however, was not so fortunate as the English in having the custom abolished. Not till 1759 the *Comédie Française*, by the liberality of a noble playgoer, succeeded in introducing a reasonable arrangement of the stage, by which spectators were entirely excluded from it. Comp. Ad. Jullien : *Les spectateurs sur le Théâtre*, Paris, 1875.

Henslowe, as we have seen, was no liberal employer, and was very eager to take advantage of every opportunity as it offered, and at a period when there was no particularly strong competition between the theatres, we find him paying ridiculously small sums to the companies employed by him. In fact he did not buy the pieces himself, but acted as a kind of agent between the authors and the actors. We see from the complaints lodged against him by his company (comp. above, p. 88) that they had "paid him upwards of £200 for play-books, and yet he refuses to give us the manuscripts of any of them."[1] He kept them, indeed, as security for the debt in which the actors stood to him.

By his extensive system of loans Henslowe kept authors as well as actors in constant dependence on himself, which enabled him to exercise a considerable pressure on the price of plays. In 1598 we find him paying Drayton, Dekker and Chettle £4 and 5 shillings in full payment for a piece with the title *Famos wares of Henry the fyrste and the prynce of Walles.*[2] Nor did the unfortunate Dekker—who, it is true, spent half his life in the debtor's prison—receive more for his *Phaeton*, while he was paid five pounds for his *The Triplicity of Cuckolds.* Before the year 1600 the ordinary price seems to have been six or seven pounds, and in Henslowe's account-books down to this date it nowhere exceeds eight pounds.

By the sale of his piece the author entirely gave up

---

[1] Articles of oppression against Mr Hinchlowe, comp. the *Alleyn Papers*, p. 81.

[2] Henslowe's *Diary*, p. 120.

his right to the possession of it, and it belonged for ever
to the company. The actors might have it altered if
they found that it no longer suited the taste of the time,
and as the manuscript belonged to them, the author
could not have it printed without the permission of the
company. The many pirated editions which nevertheless
appeared, without the consent of authors and actors,
were picked up through the ear in the theatre and
taken down in shorthand,[1] whereby, of course, the text
became utterly defective. Against pirate editors the
authors and actors had no other remedy than to pay
them for omitting to publish the piece. And that
this was really done we see from an entry in Henslowe's
Diary, which runs thus : "Lent unto Robart Shawe,
the 18 of marche 1599, to geve unto the printer, to
staye the printing of patient gresell, the some of
xxxxs."[2]

This piece, by the by, cost the old stage-manager
£10, 10s.,[3] and on the whole, about the year 1600, we
notice an increase in the fees. While down to this
period the average payment is £6, it now rises as high
as £11. This was what Ben Jonson and Dekker
received in August 1599 for their sensational play
Page of Plymouth, a tragedy, the plot of which was
taken from a crime recently committed. While Hens-

---

[1] " Some by stenography drew
The plot, put it in print, scarce one word true."
Thom. Heywood : *Pleasant Dialogues and
Dramas* (1637), quoted by Collier ;
English Dramatic Poetry, iii. p. 193.

[2] Henslowe's *Diary*, p. 167.

[3] Not £9, 10s. as stated by Collier in the introduction to his *Diary*, p.
xxv. ; comp. *Diary*, pp. 158 and 162.

lowe's *Diary* never shows a higher price than this eleven pounds, we see from letters written to him by authors— published among the *Alleyn Papers*—that about 1613 the price rose again, no doubt on account of the eager competition between the companies, especially those of the King and of Prince Henry. From the earlier letter from Robert Daborne, quoted above (p. 87), we learned that elsewhere he had received £20 for his pieces, but that Henslowe beat him down to £12, besides the surplus of the second day's performance. In another letter of June 25th, 1613, which is also very characteristic, he writes as follows :—

"Mr Hinchlow, I perceave y^u think I will be behind with my Tragoedy ; if soe, y^u might worthely account me dishonest ; indeed for thear good and myne own I have took extraordynary payns with the end, and alterd one other scean in the third act, which they have now in parts. For y^e Arreighnment, if you will please to be my $paym^t$, as for the other, they shall have it ; if not, try my Tragoedy first, and as y^t proves, so deal with me ; in the mean, my necessity is such y^t I must use other means to be furnisht upon it. Before God, I can have £25 for it, as some of y^e company know ; but such is my much debt to y^u, y^t so long as my labors may pleasure them, and y^u say ye word, I am wholy yours to be

"ever commaunded,

"ROB. DABORNE.

"I pray, S^r, if y^u resolv to do this curtesy for ye company, let me have 40s more tell we seale

"25 June, 1613   pade to Mr Daborne XXs."

We nowhere find an instance of a higher fee than the £25 which is mentioned here, and which, after all, may not have existed anywhere but in Daborne's poetic fancy. To this, of course, must sometimes be added the net proceeds of a performance, which might increase the profit considerably. If the play was particularly successful, it seems to have been the custom for the author to receive a small additional gratuity. At any rate, we find some—not many—such entries in Henslowe's accounts. Thus Thomas Dekker received ten shillings "over and above his price" for his play *Medicine for a Curst Wife*,[1] and John Day and others the same sum, which seems to have been the customary amount.

But though the authors' fees were but small, the managers had another item of expense, which was not inconsiderable, at least compared with the modern state of things. This was the tribute to the Censor.

King Henry the Eighth had in his time created an office, the incumbent of which was called "The Master of the Court Revels," and this functionary was entrusted with the critical examination of all the plays which were to be performed. Each play was to be "licensed" by the Master, and he was at liberty to strike out any passages according to his own judgment, or to forbid the performance altogether. For his trouble in perusing the plays and for striking out scandalous passages, particularly "oaths, profanenesses and obscenities," besides, of course, political indiscretions and attacks on particular persons, the Master of the Revels fixed a fee which at

[1] Henslowe's *Diary*, p. 240.

first does not seem to have been exorbitant. It is clear that in 1591 Mr Edmund Tylney, who occupied the post of Censor from 1578 to 1610, received no more than five shillings for each new or revived play.[1] But the great arbitrary power which he possessed in his relations with the managers rendered it easy for him to increase his fees; already in 1592 we find him charging 6sh. 8d., and in 1597 we find in Henslowe's account-book several consecutive receipts of the following kind: "Received the daie and yeare [May 31st, 1597] above written, by me Robert Johnson, to the use of the M[r.] of the Revells, of Phillippe Henslaye, the fulle and whole some of fortie shillinges, dew for this presente monthe aforesaide."[2]

The Master, then, had gradually managed to get a monthly tribute of £2 besides the fee for each play, for we must not imagine that this remuneration had stopped; on the contrary, it had been raised to seven shillings, which item of expense, however, the cunning Henslowe seems to have transferred to the actors, judging by the following entry in his book of the same year: "Lent unto Thomas Dowton, for the company to paye to the M[r] of the Revells for lysensynge of II boockes, XIIIIs; abated to Dawton Vs, so reaste 2."

It must be borne in mind, of course, that the Master received an equal sum from each of the more important managers—i.e. of four companies at least—which makes £12; besides seven shillings for at least two plays monthly of the same four companies, which comes to about £3. And all this money the Master received for the service he rendered to authors and actors for striking out

[1] Henslowe's *Diary*, pp. 18 ff.   [2] *Ibid.*, p. 79.

"oaths and profanenesses" in their plays; for his court-function he received a separate fee.

However, this monthly income, which to outsiders would seem very large in proportion to the work, was but small compared with the sums which later incumbents of the office were enabled to extort from the actors.

One of these, Sir Henry Herbert, Master of the Revels from 1623 to 1662, has left a number of most curious accounts, which prove that he "improved" much upon his predecessors in the way he increased the profits of the post. He can make money out of everything, and he reckons only in pounds; we never read anything about shillings. He charges £2 for reading a new play, £1 for an old one; £4 a week from each company; besides the net proceeds of one performance in the summer and one in the winter, fixed at £100 each, and gratuities at Christmas and at Lent of £3 each. Altogether his profits from the theatres can scarcely have been less than what in our time would equal about £3900 a year. According to his own calculation, they were even considerably higher when, in 1662, to his great and very natural annoyance, the post of Censor was abolished.

At all times this office has had its comic aspect, though perhaps the holder has often been unconscious of the fact, and Sir Henry Herbert does not fail to place himself in an amusing light by his notes, which are both naïve and consequential, and in which the offence he takes at wicked authors, his veneration of royalty, his self-satisfaction and his joy at the abundant flow of fees, are mixed up in the drollest manner.

We will quote a few passages, which will succeed, better than any long description, in placing us at once in the midst of the theatrical life of those times, at all events in one corner of it.

In the year 1633 he receives for perusal a play entitled *The Young Admiral* by James Shirley, a very productive and popular author. It obtains his gracious approval, because it is free from "oaths, prophaness or obsceanes," and he thinks it may "serve for a patterne to other poetts, not only for the bettring of maners and language, but for the improvement of the quality, which has received some brushings of late."

"When," he adds, with the unshakable faith of literary censors in the importance of their own judgments, "Mr Shirley has read this approbation, I know it will encourage him to pursue this beneficial and cleanly way of poetry, and when other poetts heare and see his good success, I am confident they will imitate the original for their own credit, and make such copies in this harmless way, as shall speak them masters in their art, at the first sight, to all judicious spectators. . . ."

"I have entered this allowance, for direction to my successor, and for example to all poetts, that shall write after the date hereof."[1]

Immediately after, he tells us that "at the old Exchange" he has met the leading man of "Queen's company," the actor Beeston, who has evidently courted his favour, for Sir Herbert adds : "He gave my wife a payre of gloves that cost him at least twenty shillings."

In the previous year another play by Shirley, *The*

[1] Malone : *Historical Account*, p. 293.

Ball, had been acted ; but this piece had not been to Herbert's taste at all, for it contained portraits of many lords and courtiers, which evidently had not been discovered by the Censor while perusing the play ; he writes : . . . "ther were divers personated so naturally, both of lords and others of the court, that I took it ill and would have forbidden the play, but that Biston promiste many things which I found faulte withall should be left out, and that he would not suffer it to be done by the poett any more, who deserves to be punished ; and the first that offends in this kind, of poets or players, shall be sure of publique punishment." [1]

In Ben Jonson's *Tale of a Tub* he strikes out the whole part of Vitruvius Hoop at the instigation of Inigo Jones, the royal scene-painter, who in this character saw a satire on himself. His reward for this is £2.

Now and then, nevertheless, we see his literary verdicts reversed by King Charles I. himself, which causes him to write the following amusing note : " This morning, being the 9th of January 1633, the Kinge was pleasd to call mee into his withdrawinge chamber to the windowe, wher he went over all that I had croste in Davenant's play-booke, and allowing of *faith* and *slight* to be asseverations only and no oathes, markt them to stande, and some other few things, but in the greater part allowed of my reformations. This was done upon a complaint of Mr Endymion Porter in December."

" The Kinge is pleased to take *faith, death, slight*, for asseverations and no oaths, to which I doe humbly submit as my master's judgment ; but under favour

---

[1] Malone : *Historical Account*, p. 292.

conceive them to be oaths, and enter them here, to declare my opinion and submission." [1]

Another time he himself applies to the King about a play by Massinger, one of the last which this author wrote.   Its title was *The King and the Subject*, and we find in it a speech, in which Don Pedro, King of Spain, addresses his subjects in the following words :—

> Monys? We'le rayse supplies what ways we please
> And force you to subscribe to blanks, in which
> We'le mulct you as wee shall thinke fitt.   The Cæsars
> In Rome were wise, acknowledginge no lawes
> But what their swords did ratifye, the wives
> And the daughters of the senators bowinge to
> Their wills, as deities. . . .

At a time when King and subjects did not live on the best of terms with one another, we cannot wonder that these words caused some alarm to a royal censor, though he may have been amply paid by the actors for showing indulgence.   Even His Majesty, on perusing the play, put a mark against the passage, adding in his own handwriting: " This is too insolent, and to be changed."

A few years later his subjects were guilty of the still greater and quite irreparable insolence of decapitating their King.

In the notes of these Masters of the Revels, though they treat almost exclusively of dramatic pieces, it is most interesting to notice how little the name of Shakespeare predominates over the names of the other

---

[1] Malone, *Historical Account*, p. 295.

dramatists. Sir Herbert certainly was no artist, nor can we suppose him to have been a man of particularly refined taste ; still, he came almost daily in contact with all the dramatic celebrities of his time, and his office obliged him to acquaint himself with the entire dramatic literature. If, indeed, so shortly after his death, the fame of Shakespeare as something unique, something of which the value towered considerably above that of his contemporaries, had entered into the minds of the people and been fixed there, as modern biographers try to make us believe, we should certainly have discovered it in the way his dramas are mentioned by the censor. But these records do not give the slightest indication that he held such a peculiar position, or rather, we distinctly see that the poet's crown, which we have bestowed as a humble tribute on Shakespeare, would in those days have caused the greatest astonishment. Mr Shakespeare was a clever playwright like so many others, his comedies pleased like those of so many others. *Cymbeline* receives the character " well liked by the King," but Fletcher's *Loyal Subject* is "very well liked by the King." *The Taming of the Shrew* is only "liked." *A Winter's Tale* is mentioned in the following terms as an old half forgotten play.[1] . . . " An olde playe called *Winter's Tale*, formerly allowed of by Sir George Burke, and likewyse by mee on Mr Heminge his worde that there was nothing profane added or reformed, thog the allowed booke was missinge, and therefore I returned it without a fee, this 19th of August 1623."

Shakespeare's biographers tell us that his plays were

---

[1] Malone, *Historical Account*, p. 288.

King Charles the First's "companions in his solitude"—
the expression is taken from Milton[1]—but in Herbert's
records we read that the same king says about *The
Gamester*, by Shirley, that it was the best play he had
seen for seven years, and at that time he had seen many
of Shakespeare's.

It seems clear, not only from this testimony, but from
a great deal of other evidence, and particularly from the
whole tone and manner in which Shakespeare and his
contemporaries are mentioned, that even if his supremacy
was acknowledged by the few, especially among authors
and actors, even if he was both appreciated by experts
and popular among the people at large, he by no means
stood as the one star; and neither during his life-time
nor shortly afterwards were people aware of the enormous
distance in artistic genius between him and the best of
his contemporaries, a distance which in later times
placed him on an almost supernatural summit of lonely
majesty.

When the Civil War broke out in 1642, and all play-
houses were closed, the office of Censor naturally ceased
to exist.   At the accession of Charles II. in 1660, Sir
Henry Herbert still held the office of Master of the
Revels, and when the theatres reopened, he resumed
his high claims on the managers.   But they were recal-
citrant and would pay no longer.   After a hard struggle,
with many interesting lawsuits, on which, however, we
will not enter more particularly here, since they belong
to another period, the king sided with the actors and
deprived the master of his censorial authority over the

[1] *Iconoclastes*, 1690, pp. 9 ff., quoted in Lee's *Life of Shakespeare*.

plays, and thereby of every pecuniary claim on the theatres.

One of the last items of payment which Sir Henry entered in his book is £2, which he claimed (in June 1642) for a new play, " which I burnte for the ribaldry and offense that was in it."

IV

Actors' Fees and Profits of the Theatres—Great Theatrical Celebrities and Minor Actors—What Shakespeare Earned—Magnificence of Costumes—Actors' Contracts.

It is by no means easy to form a clear idea of the conditions regarding the payment of actors during the Shakespearean period, and the sources at hand are far from throwing a full light on the matter. So much, however, is evident, that the system of payment was the same which prevailed in Italy and France—where, perhaps, it originated—the share-holding or *sociétaire* system, which in an essentially unaltered form is still prevalent in the *Comédie Française* in Paris.

The actors were sharers in the theatre, *i.e.* after deducting the current expenses they shared the proceeds among them, at first probably in the simplest way, as in France, where after the performance the account was made up at once, and the net proceeds divided. But afterwards the distribution was made in a much more business-like manner.

The sharers in the proceeds were the proprietor of the theatre, who probably possessed the largest number of shares, the permanent members of the company, and, for a time at all events, the Master of the Court Revels. No shares were due to the following : the inferior actors, who, as nowadays, are engaged by the week ; the gatherers, who served also as supers ; the book-holder or prompter, who had to look after the actors' entrances and to give them their cues and properties, if necessary ("prompting," in our sense of the word, was out of the question in the time of Shakespeare); the stage-keeper, who kept the stage in order, strewed it with rushes before the beginning of the performance, picked up the rotten apples and oranges which might have been thrown at the actors during the performance, and let stools to the spectators who were placed on the stage.

All these subordinate functionaries were called by the one name of hirelings, and were paid either by the company or by the proprietor.[1] What salary they received I have not been able to make out. It seems as if a subordinate actor who, as we remember, was not a shareholder, received one shilling a day. On the whole, the position of these third-rate or fourth-rate actors was no doubt very humble, and to become a sharer was the aim and end of every young actor. Among the *Alleyn Papers* we find a letter from such an actor, who is still playing for a fixed weekly payment, which he even does not always receive. Now he has an opportunity of going to the Continent with a travelling company, and asks his rich and celebrated comrade, Edward Alleyn, for a loan to redeem his pawned clothes. This little letter is very characteristic and full of life. It runs as follows :—

[1] Compare above p. 88.

" Mr Allen, I commend my love and humble duty to you, geving you thankes for y^r great bounty bestoed upon me in my sicknes, when I was in great want : God blese you for it.   Sir, this it is, I am to go over beyond the seeas w^t Mr Browne and the company, but not by his meanes, for he is put to half a shaer, and to stay hear, for they are all against his going ; now, good Sir, as you have ever byne my worthie frend, so helpe me nowe.   I have a sute of clothes and a cloke at pane for three pound, and if it shall pleas you to lend me so much to release them, I shall be bound to pray for you so long as I leve ; for if I go over, and have no clothes, I shall not be esteemd of ; and, by gods help, the first money that I gett I will send it over unto you, for hear I get nothinge, so that I leve in great poverty hear, and so humbly take my leave, prainge to god, I and my wiffe, for y^r health and mistris Allen's, which god continew.— Yo^r poor frend to command,   RICHARD JONES." [1]

The boys who acted the female parts (during this period, and as far down as 1656, no English woman mounted the boards) of course were not sharers, nor were they properly engaged ; they were simply bought by the manager, received their training—and probably board and clothes as well—of him, and were hired out to the company.   Thus in Henslowe's accounts we find the following entries :—

" Bowght my boye, Jeames Bryston, of William Augustus, player, the 18 of desembr 1597, for VIII. li " [2] ; and three years later : " Antony Jeaffes and the company doth owe unto me for my boye, Jeames Bristo, wages,

[1] *Alleyn Papers*, p. 19.   [2] Henslowe's *Diary*, p. 259.

from the 23rd of Aprell 1600 ; wch Robart Shawe hath geven his word for the paymente." [1]

When the boys were grown up and remained at the theatre acting male parts, of course they might rise to a higher position like all the others, and become distinguished sharers.   Nathaniel Field is probably the most celebrated among the child-actors of the time, and he was just one of those who afterwards rose to high distinction, and became one of the leading sharers.

About the mutual economical relations between the sharers there has been hitherto great uncertainty, confusion and contradiction among experts.   I will try to consider the matter in the light of fairly definite facts.

The first question to be settled is the approximate annual sum to which a share might amount.   And we do, as a matter of fact, possess a document which shows the average amount of such a share, a scale of fees which in 1662, by the desire of the Lord Chamberlain, was delivered to him by Sir Henry Herbert, the Master of the Court Revels.   Sir Herbert in his estimate enumerates the emoluments of his office—from 1628-1642—and one item (which both Malone and Collier seem to have overlooked in their attempts to explain the conditions of payment of the time) runs thus : " For a share from each companye four companyes of players (besides the late Kinge's Companye) valued at £100 a yeare, one yeare with another, besides the usual fees, by the yeare, £400 0s. 0d."

Sir Henry therefore reckons a £100 to be an average share.   Though we cannot altogether rely on

<hr>

[1] Henslowe's *Diary*, p. 149.

the estimate of the Master of the Court Revels—he greatly overrates the proceeds of the two benefits allowed him by fixing them at £50, while in reality they did not amount to more than £9 on an average—in this instance we have no reason to suppose that he exaggerates the amount of a full share. To be engaged with a full share was a thing which commanded some respect,[1] and the more distinguished actors, as a rule, were men of considerable means. There does not seem then to be any reason for doubting Henry Herbert's statement, especially as even in 1678 a share was as large as £300,[2] and yet at that time the shares were considerably diminished.

The second question to be asked is: how many shares were there in the Shakespearean period, and how were they distributed?

Malone supposes—though, contrary to his custom, he does not give any reason for his supposition—that there were forty shares, which he fancies were distributed in the following way: the proprietor (the *housekeeper* as he was called) received fifteen shares, the actors twenty-two, and three were spent on the purchase of new plays, costumes, etc.[3] Collier, as usual, repeats Malone's supposition without being able to throw further light on the matter.

Now, as in another place, Malone estimates the

[1] Comp., *e.g.*, *Hamlet*, iii. 2: *Hamlet*: " Would not this, sir, and a forest of feathers—if the rest of my fortunes turn Turk with me—with two Provincial roses on my razed shoes, get me a fellowship in a cry of players, sir?"
Horatio: " Half a share."
Hamlet: " A whole one, I."
[2] Comp. the complaint of Charles Killigrew and several of his actors against Dryden, in which they reproach him with pocketing his share and a quarter amounting to £300 or £400, but writing no plays.—Malone's *Historical Account*, p. 191, n. 9.
[3] Malone's *Historical Account*, pp. 188 ff.

average net proceeds of a performance at £9, and the average annual number of performances at 200, the total annual income of a theatre would not be more than £1800, and the salary of a full-share actor not more than £45, which undoubtedly is very little, even considering the high value of money in those days, and much too little to allow of the leading actors becoming men of considerable means.

I believe Malone to be in error.   Among the *Alleyn Papers* we find the draught of a contract (of 1608) between Thomas Henslowe and Edward Alleyn on the one side and the distinguished actor Thomas Dowton on the other, according to which Dowton is engaged to act in "The Fortune" Theatre, and is to receive "an eighth part of a quarter of all . . . net proceeds in money" at the said theatre.   By "net proceeds" is understood the profits after deducting the daily expenditure on officers and subordinate members of the staff, on light, where light was used, in short on the regular and daily recurring demands on the budget. These expenses, according to Sir Herbert's accounts, amounted to about £2, 5s. a-day.[1]   In order to obtain this thirty-second share Dowton had first to pay down in ready money £27, 10s. "in lawful English coin," and, in addition, 10s. per annum as long as the contract lasted.   He further engaged himself to undertake a thirty-second share of the expenses for repairs, etc., at

---

[1] "The kinges company with a generall consent and alacritye have given mee the benefitt of too dayes in the yeare, the one in summer, thother in winter, to bee taken out of the second daye of a revived playe, att my owne choyse.   The housekeepers have likewyse given their shares, their dayly charge only deducted, which comes to some 2l. 5s. this 25 May, 1628."

the theatre. Finally, as a sharer he was not allowed to discontinue acting unless prevented by illness, and of course he had to give up every right of acting in any other theatre in London, or within two miles' distance from it, without the permission of Henslowe or Alleyn.

I think I may conclude from this contract that in Henslowe's and Alleyn's theatres there were thirty-two shares, and I suppose—for reasons which I shall explain presently—that of these shares the proprietors themselves retained eight, a fourth part of the net proceeds. Of the remaining twenty-four shares four were probably put aside as a reserve fund for paying for the répertoire, etc., and the remaining twenty shares may have been divided between the actors, not all of whom, however, received a full share, since we hear both of three quarters and of halves.

According to this calculation, a London theatre of the first rank at that time would give average receipts of £3200, in addition to the £2 and 5s., which were the current daily expenses. If we fix the annual number of performances at 240, which is certainly not too many, as they went on summer and winter, we get the average proceeds of about £13 from each performance. And this is not too much,[1] though Malone reckons only an average of £9. But his average receipts are calculated on the benefits of the Master of the Revels, which were all only performances of second-rate value, without a

[1] The £25 which Mr Sidney Lee (*Life of W. Shakespeare*, p. 161), without proper calculation, mentions as the daily proceeds of "The Globe" Theatre, is decidedly too much, and there is not the slightest indication to show that "The Globe" could hold 2000 people.

single new play or "first night," which must necessarily give too low an amount for the average proceeds.

I have calculated from Henslowe's *Diary* that his daily receipts were about thirty shillings;[1] with an annual share of £100 and 240 performances a year, each sharer would receive daily about eight shillings. It is most probable, indeed, that Henslowe held four shares out of the thirty-two, while Alleyn, as fellow-proprietor, held the other four. But Alleyn was, moreover, a very popular actor, who played all the chief parts in the repertoire. As such he may also have had a number of shares. In Ben Jonson's *Poetaster* we read of an actor who is called "Seven shares and a half," and I fancy that no one but Edward Alleyn can be meant. In the scene between Tucca, the swaggering captain, and the actor Histrio, Tucca says: "Well, now fare thee well, my honest penny-biter. Commend me to seven shares and a half, and remember to-morrow.—If you lack a service, you shall play in my name, rascals; but you shall buy your own cloth, and I'll ha' two shares for my countenance."[2]

"Fleay has shown[3] that the actors who appear in *The Poetaster* belong partly to "The Fortune," partly to "The Rose" Theatres, both under the management of Alleyn and Henslowe. The latter, as we know, possessed four shares, so Seven-and-a-half-share can only mean Alleyn. Whether Alleyn really was in

[1] During one short period, which I leave out of consideration here, Henslowe evidently had a much smaller share. It was at the time when his company acted together with the Lord Chamberlain's Servants (comp. p. 60). During that period his average share was only a little more than nine shillings.

[2] Ben Jonson : *The Poetaster*, Act iii., Scene 4.

[3] Fleay : *The English Drama*, i. 368.

possession of so considerable a portion must remain an open question. The above somewhat uncertain proof is the only one I have been able to find. At any rate, Alleyn became a very rich man, and must, therefore, have had a very large income. The seven-and-a-half shares represent in modern money about £4500.

It is true that Alleyn was by far the richest of all the actors of his time. And, on the whole, it must be borne in mind that this calculation only applies to the best actors of the best companies. The inferior companies, of course, gained less, as the shares were necessarily smaller.[1] Only a first-rate actor in a first-rate company could have a salary of £100 a year, equal to about £800 in our time. And the very few who rose above this income only did so on account of particular circumstances, by being part-proprietors of the theatre, by holding shares in several theatres and places of amusement simultaneously, by being both authors and actors, or in some other way.

In the theatrical enterprises of Burbage the conditions were arranged in the same way as in Henslowe's, though we have reason to suppose that in the former the terms were more profitable to the actors as well as to the authors; for, evidently, the brothers Burbage were

---

[1] Mr Lee in his work on Shakespeare quoted above (p. 159 libr. ed.) asserts that we know of no actor's fee lower than three shillings a day; but the reader will have gathered from the above statements that this is a mistake. On the whole, Mr Lee, as I think, represents the conditions as a good deal more brilliant than they really were. Because men like Alleyn, Shakespeare, Burbage, and Condell, who, besides being excellent actors, were economical and energetic men of business, left a good deal of property, we must not forget that even men like Ben Jonson and Nathaniel Field were constantly in money difficulties; nor must we leave out of consideration the large number, who stood far beneath the high level of these men, struggling hard to earn the daily shilling.

scarcely as skilled as Henslowe and Alleyn in the art of making capital out of the artists who worked for them.

Nevertheless, the celebrated Richard Burbage left a very considerable fortune, if not quite so large a one as Alleyn's. It is valued by a contemporary at £300 in annual interest on landed property.[1]

Our knowledge about the conditions of the share system in the three Burbage theatres, " The Theatre," " The Globe " and " Blackfriars," is drawn from a series of letters which Halliwell-Phillipps brought to light in 1870, letters which date from the year 1635, and give us some insight into a struggle between the non-sharing actors Robert Benfield, Heliard Swanston and Thomas Pollard on the one side, and the sharers in " The Globe " and " Blackfriars," among them the actors Shancke, Taylor, Robinson and Lowin on the other.[2]

What we learn through these letters confirms what we have gathered from Henslowe's and other papers. We see that at that time " The Globe " was divided into sixteen and " Blackfriars " into eight shares—which equals the thirty-two shares with Henslowe and Alleyn. The sixteen shares of " The Globe " are distributed among six hands only, of which, moreover, only four are actors, whereas the bookseller, Cuthbert Burbage and the widow, Mrs Condell, have five and a half shares between them.

[1] In a letter from John Chamberlain to Sir Dudley Carlton (State Papers quoted by Malone) we read : " The funeral [of the Queen] is put off to the 29th of next month, to the great hinderance of our players, which are forbidden to play so long as her body is above ground ; one special man among them is lately dead, and hath left, they say, better than 300 l. land."

[2] All these letters are printed in Halliwell-Phillipps's *Outlines*, 3rd ed. pp. 539-551.

The discontented non-sharing actors complain of these conditions to the Earl of Pembroke, who, at the time, was Lord Chamberlain at the court of King Charles I. They wish to become sharers, and think it unreasonable that so large a number of shares should be in the hands of men who are not actors themselves, but merely reap the fruits of their toil and trouble. How wrong these conditions are they prove by showing that the sharers in "The Globe" have a daily profit of two shillings a share, while the actor's part does not exceed three shillings. This, as we see, harmonises closely with our above calculation.

These statements, it is true, are contradicted by the opposing party, who assert that the complaining actors have gained £180 each during the last year, which is admitted to be double of what they have gained hitherto; but even half of £180 gives a considerably larger daily sum than three shillings.

Now, even if both parties exaggerate, it is evident that the sharer was much better off than the ordinary actor, for otherwise the latter would not have coveted this position as eagerly as the former tried to prevent him from obtaining it.

Cuthbert Burbage's defence of the existing order of things is very interesting, as it shows us how the circumstances gradually developed.

His father, he tells us, was the very first builder of theatres, and "The Theatre" cost him many hundred pounds, which he borrowed at interest. "The players that lived in those first times" (that is about sixty years before Cuthbert writes this), "had only the profitts arising from the dores, but now the players receave all the commings in at the dores to themselves and halfe the galleries from the housekepers." [1]

We see that old James Burbage left to his actors the regular entrance fee, which was collected at the door; but the extra amount which was paid for sitting in the boxes and the gallery, "the House," as it was called, he took for himself, for the house was his own and built at his own expense.

Afterwards, however, this distribution went a little too much in favour of the owner. The most distinguished and indispensable actors were included among the sharers, and, with Burbage, the whole company received, besides the entrance fees, half of the proceeds of "the House." But, as the three complaining actors point out, from this sum were deducted "all expenses for hirelings, apparel, poets, light and all other expenses of the play-houses." On the other hand, all repairs of the building naturally devolved on the owners.

What tempts us most in making these financial researches is to find out the financial condition of Shakespeare.

It has always been well known that Shakespeare was a man of means when he died. That he had honestly gained his little fortune by means of his art, his biographers ought to have assumed as a foregone conclusion, instead of searching for mysterious sources of income, or inventing supernaturally liberal patrons.

Indeed, it was not as an author—at any rate not in a direct way—that he enriched himself. If Shakespeare

[1] Halliwell-Phillipps, *Outlines*, p. 549.

were to rise from the grave at this moment and receive the fees for his plays from all parts of the world, he would probably take many times more in one season than the amount which his works brought him throughout his whole life-time. We have seen that the author's fees were but small. Ben Jonson, in his conversations with Drummond, asserts that he did not gain more than £200 from his plays altogether,[1] and even if Shakespeare gained a good deal more, the direct proceeds of his works cannot have been considerable. But, indirectly, his dramatic works were a capital which brought him abundant interests as an actor and afterwards as proprietor, since their great popularity attracted crowds to the theatre in which he was concerned, and thus procured for himself and his comrades a large annual profit.

It would be impossible, of course, to give an exact account of Shakespeare's income ; still, with the information we possess about theatrical matters, we can make an approximate calculation.

That his old fellow-townsmen at Stratford considered him a man of considerable means as early as 1598 appears from a number of letters concerning loans and purchases, dating from that time.[2] Yet this must have been his least prosperous period. Between 1590 and 1599, indeed, he wrote nineteen dramatic works, but before 1600 the price of these plays was but low. Henslowe, as we have heard, at that time did not pay more than £11. Though Burbage may have given rather more, and though there may from time to time have been

---

[1] D. Laing : *Ben Jonson's Conversations with Drummond*, p. 35.
[2] See Sidney Lee : *Life of Shakespeare*, pp. 154 ff.

a benefit and a small extra fee of ten shillings, we cannot fix the average payment for these nineteen plays at more than £12, which makes an annual profit of £25 during the first nine years of his theatrical career. His actor's share in the entrance fees of " The Theatre " and other play-houses may be fixed at £75, if we allow him a double share, and suppose a share to have been three shillings a day, and the days of performance 240 in number. To this must be added the performances at Court and at the country seats of the noblemen, which might yield about £15 a year, amounting altogether to a total of £115.

Though this is no exorbitant sum, it is sufficiently large to justify his townspeople in calling him a man of considerable means.

But after 1599 his income must have increased very much. Higher prices began to be paid for plays, and, what was more important, " The Globe " Theatre was built, and Shakespeare became part - owner of this house, together with Condell, Heminge, Phillipps and others.[1]

As we know, the enterprise was divided into sixteen shares. Of these the brothers Burbage no doubt held four (in 1635 Cuthbert himself had 3½ shares). The remaining twelve were probably distributed among six principal actors, two shares to each. A share in " The Globe" (which was double the value of one in " The Fortune ") may reasonably be fixed at £200. Besides this he may have had his share of the admission fees, though that does not absolutely follow, and this may not

---

[1] Cuthbert Burbage's letter to the Earl of Pembroke, Halliwell-Phillipps, *Outlines*, p. 549.

have exceeded the amount of one share. Altogether his profits as an actor may have amounted to about £450.

During the period from 1599 to 1611—with the latter year Shakespeare closed his theatrical career—he wrote seventeen plays. He certainly did not receive less than £25 for any of them, as that was the sum which an insignificant author like Robert Daborne claimed to be able to earn from " The Globe " Theatre (see above, p. 126); this would make £425 for the seventeen plays, or during the last twelve years an average sum of £35 per annum. To this may be added the proceeds of Court performances and authors' benefits, which, without the slightest exaggeration, may be supposed to have brought him in £30 a year. According to this calculation Shakespeare must have earned an annual sum of about £515 during the best twelve years of his career.[1]

It may be said in general that during the Elizabethan period the English actors as a class were comparatively well off, and that their economical condition, as well as the consideration which they enjoyed, went on steadily improving down to the time of the Civil War. We possess several pieces of evidence which show that other classes looked with a certain jealousy on the wealthy theatrical class, and thought it absurd that these vagabonds, who not many years previously were obliged to drag themselves along carrying their baggage on their

---

[1] Mr Sidney Lee has made a similar calculation (*Life of Shakespeare*, pp. 154-162), and has arrived at a similar, if somewhat higher, result. I cannot, however, agree with him in the details. At all events, we cannot fix an ordinary actor's share at £180, as our only source (John Shancke's letter to Lord Pembroke, *Outlines*, p. 546) expressly mentions this sum as double the amount which actors generally received.

backs, were now to be seen riding ostentatiously through
the streets on smart horses and in showy silk clothes.

In an anonymous University play of 1601, *The Return
from Parnassus*, this anger vents itself in the following
verses by the poor student who wrote them :—

> " Vile world that lifts them up to high degree
> And treads us down in grovelling misery !
> England affords these glorious vagabonds,
> That carried erst their fardels on their backs,
> Coursers to ride on through the gazing streets,
> Sweeping it in their glaring satin suits,
> And pages to attend their master-ships :
> With mouthing words that better wits have framed
> They purchase lands, and now esquires are made." [1]

The last lines most likely allude to Edward Alleyn, who
at this period was probably the only actor who rose beyond
the usual style of theatrical artists by exchanging the title
of gentleman for that of esquire (possessor of an estate).

It is probable that a similar bitter sally against actors,
which is found in a small pamphlet of about 1606,
" Ratsey's Ghost," is also partly directed against Alleyn.
Gamaliel Ratsey was a well-known highwayman, who
had forced a travelling company of actors to play
gratuitously to him. In return he gives the following
rule of life to one of the actors, who is on his way to
London, where Ratsey advises him to seek his fortune :
" There (says he) thou shalt learn to be frugal (for
players were never so thrifty as they are now about
London), and feed upon all men ; to let none feed upon

---

[1] *The return from Parnassus*, Act. v., Sc. i.

thee; to make thy hand a stranger to thy pocket, thy heart slow to perform thy tongue's promise; and when thou feelest thy purse well lined, *buy thee some place of lordship in the conntry*, that, growing weary of playing, thy money may there bring thee to dignity and reputation; then thou needest care for no man; no, not for them that before made thee proud with speaking their words on the stage." [1]

The last lines cannot properly apply to Alleyn, who was born in London; they are much more appropriate to Shakespeare, who had indeed come to London poor and without employment in order to seek his fortune, and who by this time—about 1606—was very wealthy.

Some of the Puritan writings also mention the wealth and magnificence of the actors, and especially their extravagance in dress. We mentioned above poor Richard Jones, who, having to live upon one shilling a day, which he did not get, attempts to borrow £3 to redeem his clothes, for "if he has no clothes, he will not be respected." Clothes, on the whole, were a very important point with actors. Yet, in the portraits we know of Elizabethan actors, they appear by no means dressed with excessive magnificence, though these likenesses represent the very richest and most distinguished theatrical personages of the time, such as Edward Alleyn, Richard Burbage, Shakespeare and Field. Among these, Burbage (comp. fig. 15), the celebrated stage-hero and wealthy proprietor, is even modestly dressed; Alleyn (comp. fig. 13), the circus-manager and millionaire-actor, is decently but simply dressed, like an

---

[1] *The Alleyn Papers*, Introduction, p. 10.

honest citizen.   Shakespeare appears in somewhat more
elegant attire, with a touch of the nobleman, especially
in the Droeshout portrait (fig. 10) and in the terra-cotta
bust (fig. 14), yet without the slightest showiness or
extravagance.   Finally, Nathaniel Field (fig. 16), who,
though not rich, was a very fashionable and, no doubt,
very smart actor, wore a rather odd but apparently not
very expensive indoor suit.

On the stage, however, we know that there was a
magnificent display of apparel.   It is well known that
the stage costumes did not differ in cut from the ordinary
dresses of the time.   There was no more attempt during
the Renaissance period than there had been during the
Middle Ages to adapt the costumes to historical requirements ; all plays alike were acted in contemporary dress.
In this respect, however, distant countries weighed a
little more in the scale than different periods, and, as in the
Middle Ages, clumsy attempts were made to represent
fantastic costumes, Mahometan or Turkish, for instance.
Attention was also paid to the different fashions of
civilised countries ; thus in Henslowe and Alleyn's list of
apparel we read of " French hose and Spanish doublet."

This habit of playing everything in the same kind
of costume naturally very much curtailed the wardrobe
expenses.   On the other hand, the costumes in themselves were exceedingly expensive, so much so that a
fine costume actually cost more than one of Shakespeare's
tragedies.

In the *Alleyn Papers* (p. 12) we find a long legal
document drawn up in minute detail, which for a payment of £20, 10s. transfers to the brothers John and

Edward Alleyn—a cloak! It is true, this garment was of velvet, elaborately embroidered in silver and gold, lined with black and gold striped satin ; still £20 seems a large sum to pay for a stage-cloak, considering that this, as we know, was looked upon as an exceedingly high price for a play.[1]

And this sum does not even seem to have been uncommonly high for a costume. Another contract in the same collection tells us that John Alleyn paid £16 for " one cloke of velvett with a cape imbrothered with gold, pearles and red stones, and one roabe of cloth of golde." [2]

The Renaissance in England was a period of imitation, like our own time. The materials in which the actors appeared were genuine and expensive, not cheap silks and tinsel. In Henslowe's *Diary* I find the following little item : " Lent unto Robert Shawe, the 26th of novembr 1597, to by viii yds of clothe of gowld, the some of fowr powndes : I saye lent for the usse of the company . . ." [3]

This would be about equal to £4 a yard nowadays, a price which would make a modern manager turn pale. And shortly after the same Robart Shawe borrows sixteen shillings (equal to about £6 nowadays) to buy "copper lace of sylver, to lace a payer of hosse for alles perce [Alice Pierce]." . . .

Between these two items we find the following entry : " Lent unto Bengemen Johnsone, the 3 of desembr 1597, upon a Booke [4] wch he has to writte for us befor crysmas next after the date hereof, wch he

---

[1] *Alleyn Papers*, p. 12.   [2] *Alleyn Papers*, p. 11.
[3] Henslowe's *Diary*, p. 104.
[4] Perhaps *The Fall of Mortimer*. Compare Fleay : *English Drama*, i. 356.

showed the plotte unto the company : I saye lente in Redy money unto hime the some of XXs."

Sometimes figures speak with incisive distinctness. The draper gets £4 for eight yards of stuff, Ben Jonson receives a loan of twenty shillings for engaging himself to write a play from the 3rd to the 24th of December. So, if in other respects the stage equipment was cheap, large sums were spent in costumes, an expense which was generally defrayed by the actors themselves. Whether the costliness and well-known splendour of the dresses was always in proportion to their taste and style is another question, which Ben Jonson in his Introduction to his *Staple of News* tempts us to answer in the negative. He says there : " O *Curiosity*, you come to see who wears the new suit to-day ; whose cloath are best pen'd, whatever the part be ; which actor has the best leg and foot ; what king plays *without cuffs*, and his queen *without gloves* ; who rides post *in stockings*, and dances in *boots*." [1]

Prynne, the fanatic Puritan, also complains that the public plays were generally acted in over-expensive, effeminate, fantastic and gorgeous clothes.[2]

It only requires a superficial perusal of Alleyn's and

---

[1] Ben Jonson : *Staple of News*, Introduction. The above quotation, it seems to me, is no proof whatever that the costumes were poor at " The Globe " Theatre, as Malone thinks they were (*Historical Account*, p. 127), only that they were sometimes negligently arranged and not in harmony with the character of the part.

[2] Prynne : *Histriomastix*, p. 216. It seems to me that Malone equally alters the meaning of this passage by saying that the fanatical Prynne, who thought playgoers little better than incarnated devils, might easily take a piece of coarse stuff trimmed with tinsel for a magnificent and ungodly dress. We have seen above that the stuffs as well as the trimming were genuine and expensive enough.

Henslowe's lists of apparel and of their account-books to show us that the Puritan is not quite wrong. Among these old items of expense there is a rustling of silk and velvet and a sparkling of gold, silver and precious stones. Many a good shilling of the actors' fees was spent on the costly dresses, which afterwards went to the pawnbroker's shop, whence they had to be redeemed by "Father Henslowe." He then used to keep them as pledges for some advance of money.[1]

About the official relations of the actor with the manager, *i.e.* the proprietor, we are pretty well informed through a contract—the only one of its kind—or the *Articles*, as they were still called in theatrical language, between the actor, Robert Dawes, on the one side, and the managers, Henslowe and Meade, on the other.[2] This contract probably gives us the general formula of actors' contracts in those times, and I will here repeat its principal points, though stripping them of the involved legal attire, which renders this kind of document almost unreadable.

1. . . . the said Robert Dawes shall and will plaie with such company as the said Phillipp Henslowe and Jacob Meade shall appoynte, for and during the tyme and space of three yeares from the date hereof, for and at the rate of one whole Share, accordinge to the custome of players ; . . .

[1] Lent Thomas Dowton, to featche ii clockes owt of pane, the 2 of novmbr 1597, the some of xii li xs, for wch money these ii clockes were leafte unto me in pane, the one wasse an embrodered clocke of ashe colerd vellvet, the other a blacke vellvett clocke layd with sylke laces abowt. I saye lent unto him in Redy money xii li xs.

[2] These Articles were discovered by Malone in Dulwich College, whence, however, they have since disappeared. Fortunately they were reprinted by Malone (*Shakespeare*, by Boswell, xxi. p. 413), and afterwards in Collier's *Alleyn Papers*, pp. 75 ff.

2. . . . the said Robert Dawes shall and will at all tymes during the said term duly attend all such rehearsall, which shall the night before the rehearsall be given publickly out, and that if he the saide Robert Dawes shall at any tyme faile to come at the hower appoynted, then he shall and will pay to the said Phillipp Henslowe and Jacob Meade, their executors or assignes, Twelve pence, and if he come not before the saide rehearsall is ended, then the said Robert Dawes is contented to pay twoe shillings.

3. . . . if the said R. D. shall not every daie whereon any play is or ought to be played be ready apparrelled and—to begyn the play at the hower of three of the clock in the afternoone unles by sixe of the same Company he shall be lycensed to the contrary that then he . . . shall and will pay unto the said Phillipp and Jacob, or their assignes, three [shillings].

4. and if that he the saide Robert Dawes happen to be overcome with drinck at the tyme when he [ought to] play, by the Judgment of ffower of the said company, he shall and will pay Tenne shillings ;

5. and if he [the said R. D.] shall [faile to come] during any plaie having no lycence or just excuse of sicknes he is contended to pay Twenty shillings ;

6. the said Robert Dawes . . . doth covenant and grant to and with the said Phillipp Henslowe and Jacob Meade . . . to receave and take back . . . half parte of all such moneyes as shall be receaved at the galleries and tyring howse of such howse or howses wherein the said Robert Dawes shall play . . . towards the pa[ying] to them the saide Phillipp Henslowe and Jacob Meade

of the some of one hundred twenty and fower pounds [being the] value of the stock of apparell furnished by the same company by [to ?] the said Phillipp Henslowe and Jacob Meade . . .

7. . . . if the said Robert Dawes shall at any time after the play is ended depart or go out of the [howse] with any [of their] apparell on his body, or if the said Robert Dawes [shall carry away any propertie] belonging to the said Company . . . shall and will forfeit and pay . . . the some of ffortie pounds . . .

8. . . . it shall and will be lawfull to and for the said Phillipp Henslowe and Jacob Meade . . . to have and use the playhows so appoynted [for the said company —one day of] every fower daies, the said daie to be chosen by the said Phillipp and [Jacob] . . . on which it shall be lawful . . . to bait their bears and bulls ther, and to use their accustomed sport . . . allowing to the saide company for every such daye the some of fforty shillings. . . .

V

A First Performance at " The Globe."

IT is between two and three o'clock. There is bustle and excitement within the high wooden walls of " The Globe " Theatre.

To-day there is a first performance, and great expectations are entertained with regard to the new play. In the tiring-house the actors are nervously busy in putting on their magnificent new clothes and their wigs, and in painting their cheeks. The boys who play the female parts are pinched into tightening stays and adorned, painted and perfumed like any lady. The prompter and the stage-keeper run busily about with lists in their hands, seeing that all the properties are ready and that the musicians tune their instruments.

The Prologue is ready. He walks solemnly up and down in his black velvet cloak, a garment which is always worn by this functionary, mumbling to himself the introductory verses which he has to recite. He is a tall stately man of a distinguished appearance : the black velvet suits him, though it adds to the pallor which excitement gives to his face. He is not painted —and he rubs his cheeks to give them a little colour.

From the audience we hear the ever increasing sounds of humming and buzzing, now and then mixed with loud cries of female voices. We distinguish the words : "apples! nuts! ale! canary!"

The Prologue enters by one of the large gates at the back of the stage ; the draperies which divide it from the stage proper are drawn aside, and he looks out into the house.

There they stand, his judges yonder in the "yard," all those apprentices, soldiers and sailors, mixed up with the worst dregs of London, gamblers, pick-pockets and women of low repute, the people who, before three hours have passed, will have pronounced their twopenny verdict on the work in which he has expressed his fine soul's best feelings and thoughts. For it is he, the Prologue himself, who has written the new play.

The expensive seats, boxes and galleries, are still empty. Only a few lackeys sit yawning while occupying the places which they have taken for their employers. But the upper gallery, to which the admission is very cheap, is quite full, and a lively fire of coarse jokes is kept up between the gallery and the pit. People are playing cards; they drink, shout and cry, and a smell of food, ale, tobacco, garlic and cheap wine fills the house, and finds its way out through the opening of the roof, like smoke mounting through a chimney.

The Prologue turns up his nose contemptuously and draws back his head. At this moment there is a gentle touch on his shoulder and a voice asks kindly : " Aye, Will, how are you ? " He turns round. It is the manager, Richard Burbage, who also is ready to begin. They shake hands. " I am afraid those fellows will kill us before our time with their smell of garlic," says the Prologue, making room for Burbage, who now peeps out between the curtains.

Burbage too is dressed in black, but in the short costume of a young nobleman. He is a little shorter than Will and rather stout; his bearded face with the gentle, sensitive features and the large expressive eyes casts an inquisitive and business-like glance into the house. " Now the great people begin to come," he says, looking back over his shoulder at Will, "look how they pour in !—Look, there is young Sir Francis ; he has gone into the pit and glances along the galleries to find a place near the finest girl. I hope we shall give him something else to think of to-day ; shan't we, old Will ? " " We shall see," Will answers quietly.

In the house, boxes and galleries are filling with stately gentlemen and ladies. The gentlemen in costly silk and velvet dresses, with gold chains on their breasts, stiff Spanish collars, fine lace cuffs, high hats or low caps with flying ostrich feathers ; the ladies more gorgeous still, in tight-laced, long-pointed stays, enormous puffed sleeves, high lace collars, their towering natural, or false, hair interwoven with pearls—the natural hair was seldom sufficient for the fashionable head-dresses of the time— ears and fingers glittering with jewels, gloves with gold embroidered initials, faces bright with white and red paint, costly fragrance emanating from their persons.

Not all, however, show their faces, as most of the well-bred ladies are masked.   It is a peculiar and motley sight to see the boxes filling with all these variegated masks, wax-yellow, reddish brown, jet-black, grass-green, cherry, or apple-grey, through which the eyes cast their mysterious glances, while the bejewelled hands wave the large ostrich feather fans.

High up in the top-gallery we see the light-living company of the women of doubtful reputation.   They take great pains to conceal the class to which they belong ; some of them appear in gloomy black, like mourning widows ; others in grey linsey-woolsey, as if they were innocent country-maidens ; others again in lapelled bodices and aprons like ladies' maids, or in the guise of respectable matrons, if not in rustling silk and lace like ladies of rank.   But there is a something which betrays them all, with which they lure thoughtless lovers, who are to pay for their supper after the play : "those wanton eyes," which the Puritans dread and curse.

The house is full, the actors ready.   Only Burbage and the Prologue are in black ; most of the other performers are as variegated and gorgeous as the audience in the boxes. Through the tiring-house some young nobles are still forcing their way to the stage. They nod all round and greet the actors by their Christian names : "Good afternoon, Dick! have you something good to show us to-day?" "Aye, Will, are you afraid we shall mew at your play?" "Do you think you are a match for old Will Kemp, Bob?" They stroll on deliberately, followed by the stage-keeper, who carries their three-legged stools. They sit down, take their pipes from their pages, light them and begin smoking, at the same time greeting their acquaintances all round with grace and elegance.

The actors grumble in their beards at these gallants, who take up their room and blow tobacco smoke into their throats, but they dare not complain aloud ; the young men are too mighty and pay too well. The Prologue arranges his black velvet cloak and looks up at the musicians, who are ready holding their trumpets to their mouths. He gives the signal, and the first flourish rings through the theatre.

Everybody looks up ; people settle themselves ; the card-players in the pit make haste to finish their game before the play begins. Another flourish. The talk and noise abate. The apple-girls and other hawkers stop crying. The card-players put down their last trumps. The light-living women dart their last glance at the chosen friend. One more flourish, the third and last. All is quiet ; every eye is turned towards the curtains.

Behind them stands the Prologue, upright, but with

dry lips and trembling hands. He clenches his teeth.
" Shall I be able to-day to tame the many-headed
monster yonder?" he mutters; then with a quick
movement pulls aside the curtain, advances with a quiet
smile, and bows to the crowd.

"It is Shakespeare! look, Shakespeare!" is the
general whisper, and the S—es of this rare name hiss
through the house.   The great lords nod kindly in
acknowledgment, the apprentices and sailors in the pit
roar out a welcome to their "Will," and the ladies in
both the first and the second galleries smile insinuatingly
at their honey-sweet poet, who has written the graceful
Venus and Adonis which stands at home on their shelf
between Beaumont's *Salmacis and Hermaphroditus* and
Marston's *Pygmalion's Image.*

With a grace and dignity of his own, Shakespeare
recites the introductory verses and retires slowly,
followed by the applause of his friends.

But he has no sooner disappeared behind the
curtains than his dignity is thrown off.   In a great
hurry, and tucking up his richly folded velvet mantle,
he flies to the tiring-room.   "Right so, Willy, make
haste!" Burbage cries after him ; "you have not much
time."

And Shakespeare takes off his velvet cloak and puts
on the heavy armour, which lies ready for him.   With
white paint he gives a deadly pallor to his cheeks, he
puts on a long venerable black beard sprinkled with
silver, and with the crowned helmet on his head, he
stands there, awful, yet gentle and dignified, like a dead
man, clothed in steel and plate.   He seizes his

"truncheon," and, proud and majestic, advances a few steps, practising his voice which he tries to render deep and husky like a ghost's, and from his mouth come the following words :—

"I am thy father's spirit,
  Doom'd for a certain term to walk the night,
  And for the day confined to fast in fires,
  Till the foul crimes done in my days of nature
  Are burnt and purged away."

Then he walks quickly towards the stage. The prompter meets him with the book in his hand. "Presently, Mr Shakespeare," he whispers. Shakespeare listens. "Yes, indeed." Burbage enters with the two others. Shakespeare hears his own familiar verses :—

"The air bites shrewdly, it is very cold."

Suddenly a blast of trumpets is heard, and thundering cannon-shots frighten the spectators. From the stage the following verses are heard :—

"What does this mean, my lord?"

And the voice of Burbage replies with bitter sarcasm :—

"The King does wake to-night and takes his rouse,
  Keeps wassail, and the swaggering up-spring reels,
  And as he drains his draughts of Rhenish down,
  The kettle-drum and trumpet thus bray out
  The triumphs of his pledge."

Shakespeare smiles. He thinks of the merry stories which his old comrade, William Kemp, has told him of the drunken Danish king, Frederick II., and the festivals at Kronberg and Elsinore, . . . but it is time now ; he must enter.

He walks on, and the house is filled with horror and midnight awe.

The monster yonder with the many heads opens its thousand eyes and many mouths, and is seized with wonder and terror.

The act ends amid breathless calm, through which are heard the voices of Burbage and Shakespeare, those of the son and the dead father, low, but strained, like the trembling tones of the 'cello.

Then the applause bursts forth.   The act is ended. Up from the cellarage whence his " Swear!" has sounded gloomily through the theatre comes Shakespeare.   He hurries up to Burbage, who stands there out of breath after the fatiguing act.

They shake hands in silence, and both feel that this day they have done something good.

There is an entr'acte.   The noise and talk is resumed.   The apple-girls cry again as if Hamlet had never lost his father.   Critics discuss and criticise, the ladies flirt, and the mob drinks.   Here and there someone sits silently musing on what he has heard and seen.

Suddenly a shrill cry pierces the din.   A man is seen, who, with a smiling face, swings a bloody ear in his left hand and a knife in the other, while the original owner of the ear furiously screams, scolds and threatens. The crowd throngs round them.   But the first man stands calmly holding the ear in his hand.   " Now do be quiet, dear sir," he says ; " I sha'n't cheat you.   Give me back my purse, and here is your ear.   There now, take it and be off."

It is a pick-pocket, who has been caught red-handed. Just as he was sneaking away with his booty, his victim, discovering him, had drawn his dagger, and with a quick movement cut off his ear, "in order to get something for his money," as he says.

The poor pick-pocket is seized amid great noise and merry exclamations from the mob, and tied to a stake on the stage, where he remains during the rest of the performance, the laughing-stock of all, but scarcely to the advantage of the impression produced by the play.

Meanwhile the play pursues its course. The actors do their best, though they do not all please equally well. One of them has to endure an unpleasant hissing, which to his ears sounds like the noise of geese or the fizzing of a bottle of ale which is being uncorked. Another rouses such discontent that he is mewed at like a cat; while a third can hardly protect himself against the apples, oranges, and nutshells that are showered down upon him, and which are afterwards swept away by the stage-keeper and given to the bears in the adjoining garden.

But the great Burbage, the favourite of the public, the English Roscius, as they call him, though Roscius was a comic actor, and Burbage won his greatest laurels as a tragic, saves all by his powerful and deeply impressive acting.

And when, moreover, in the last act he shows his skill in fencing in the scene with Laertes, there is no end to the cheering. The success of *Hamlet* is secured. All leave the house pleased and touched.

" This Burbage is the devil of a fellow, and Shake-

speare too! Did you see how he fenced?" Such exclamations are heard while people throng towards the
narrow entrance, hasten down to the river and quarrel
with the sturdy watermen. The ladies declare their
opinion that the young man who played Osric was
charming, and beautifully dressed, and that the play was
very nice.

The actors also are pleased. They gather at a little
festival in " The Cardinal's Hat," where Burbage spends
thirty shillings in wine for them.

But who among them felt that on that day time had
turned a leaf in the book, which is called The Great
Deeds of the Human Mind?

HISTRIONIC ART

I

The Old School—Clowns—Richard Tarlton and his Art—William Kemp.

IT would be quite impossible to give anything like a full description of the art of acting and the individual actors of the Shakespearean period.

It is always difficult to fix the ephemeral art of the theatre on paper. In this respect, however, the last two centuries have afforded great assistance by the publication of numerous memoirs, appreciations and biographies of actors, and last, not least, by the issue of many pictorial representations of actors in their parts. This material for the historical treatment of histrionic art is ever increasing in value, so that in this new century we shall no doubt be able, with the assistance of the phonograph and the kinematograph, to call back to life the stage-heroes who have passed away, almost as easily as we can now take down from the shelf our Shakespeare or our Molière.

But in those old times material is virtually non-existent. No descriptive criticism, no autobiography, no picture of an actor's part—except a few rough wood-cuts of two clowns—assist us in throwing light on one of the most interesting periods of histrionic art. We know the names of a great number of actors ; we know something about them—where they were born, where they died and were buried, and how much money they left behind them.   But what places they occupied in the mighty literature of the time, or what was the character of their art, these are questions of which we are so hopelessly ignorant in every case that, for all we know of them, they might as well not have been born at all.

It is tragicomical to think that, while our contemporary theatrical statisticians put down and print a note each time when Mr X. is replaced by Mr G. as a servant in a quite indifferent piece, so that posterity is perfectly secured against mistakes about the theatrical careers of these gentlemen, we are completely cut off from ever learning which parts Shakespeare chose to represent in his own plays, and must content ourselves with supposing that he acted the ghost in *Hamlet*.

Any attempt, therefore, at a real description of the histrionic art of the time is bound to fail.   The following chapters do not pretend either to offer such a description, or to give a categorical list of names of the known actors, which would not agree at all with the plan of the present work.   Their object is to exhibit a few prominent types which are characteristic of some particular branches of the histrionic art.

Like the Drama, the earliest Elizabethan art of acting no doubt stood with one foot in the Middle Ages, without knowing where to put the other.   Certainly there existed in England at a very early period a kind of professional actors, but their domain was so limited and so peculiar that for a long time there did not seem to be any possibility of their further development.   With dramas properly so called, such as the great Mysteries and

Moralities, which impressed their stamp upon the Middle Ages, these artists had nothing to do.

These plays, we know, were performed by amateur citizens, who undertook the great task and carried it out to the best of their ability. Only the comic parts, which were required as a relief from the long strain on the attention of the audience, were executed by professionals, who could sing and dance, play the flute, beat the drum, cut all sorts of capers, crack jokes, or find rhymes at a moment's notice; in short, who possessed a whole ré-pertoire of jests and amusing tricks, which all required practice and training, and perhaps a talent of which, naturally, the citizen amateurs were destitute.

Thus the professional actors found themselves in a very isolated position. They stood in no connection with the serious subject of the play and the deep influence it exercised on the spectators; their business was only to divert the mind by their jokes. But though they carried these diversions to an extraordinary degree of perfection, their domain was naturally very limited. They continued to be "players of interludes." Actors, according to the modern acceptation of the word, did not exist till the time when dramatic literature passed entirely into the hands of professional artists.

But players of interludes continued to flourish through-out the Shakespearean period. These gay mediæval jugglers, half equilibrists, half "instrumentalists" (as they were called abroad), were comic in every sense of the word. They were not actors playing comic parts or representing comic characters; everything about them was ludicrous, their appearance, manners, movements and

speech.   They were by nature " the clown " or " fool " of
the Renaissance play, closely related to the ancient court-
fool, though with a more athletic training than the latter.
The modern English clown of the music-hall and the
circus is their direct descendant.

Everybody knows the beautiful passage in *Hamlet*,[1]
where the Prince, holding the old jester's skull in his
hand, philosophises on the vanity of life : " Let me
see.   Alas, poor Yorick !   I knew him, Horatio ; a
fellow of infinite jest, of most excellent fancy ; he hath
borne me on his back a thousand times ; and now, how
abhorred in my imagination it is ! my gorge rises at it.
Here hung those lips that I have kissed, I know not how
oft.   Where be your gibes now ? your gambols ? your
songs ? your flashes of merriment, that were wont to set
the table on a roar ?   Not one now to mask your own
grinning ? quite chop-fallen ?   Now get you to my lady's
chamber, and tell her, let her paint an inch thick, to this
favour she must come ; make her laugh at that."

The words are so pathetic and seem to betray such
personal feeling, that we are no doubt justified in believ-
ing that Shakespeare in his little funeral oration meant
to commemorate a certain late comrade.   In that case
he could be referring to none other than Richard Tarlton.

Tarlton was an exact type of the kind of actor we
have tried to describe above.   He is just the man—the
comedian—who half belongs to the Middle Ages and
cannot find a firm footing in the new literature ; the
jester *par excellence*, the idolised and mourned, but poor
and humble juggler, who, when Shakespeare wrote his

[1] Act v. Sc. I.

Hamlet, had been dead for a few years. The year of his death, 1588, was remembered as coinciding with that of the destruction of the Spanish Armada.

At Tarlton's death Shakespeare was twenty-four years old, and he may well have acted with him. It is not even improbable that he may have known him as a boy, and that Tarlton had really carried little Willy on his back when, as a travelling actor, he visited Stratford among other places. Of his many travels we are reminded in a collection of anecdotes, which was published after his death,[1] and which, by the by, affords no slight contribution to a knowledge of the kind of wit he possessed.

Otherwise we know little about his life. According to Fuller's "Worthies,"[2] he is supposed to have been born in Shropshire, where he kept his father's swine, and attracted the attention of a Leicester man by his clever replies. He came to London and became a water-carrier,[3] a characteristic figure in the daily life of old London, and a situation which might well afford him opportunities of exercising his wit, and extend his knowledge of human frailties.

---

[1] The date is unknown. In 1611 appeared *Tarlton's Jests, Drawn into three parts : His Court Witty Jests ; His Sound City Jests ; His Country Pretty Jests : full of Delight, Wit and honest Mirth*, 4to. After this first and still extant edition, a reprint was undertaken by Halliwell (1844) for the Shakespeare Society. But the three parts appeared separately at an earlier date.

[2] Thomas Fuller : *History of the Worthies of England*, London, MDCLXII. p. 47 (Staffordshire).

[3] According to Lord Wilson's play : *The Three Lords and Three Ladies of London*, which contains several references to Tarlton, and was performed shortly after his death.—Compare Fleay : *English Drama*, ii. 280, and Halliwell : *Tarlton's Jests*, p. 9.

He married a woman of somewhat loose habits, named Kate, and with her kept a tavern in Gracious (*i.e.* Gracechurch) Street, and at another period a public-house in Paternoster Row.[1]   It is not known when he became an actor, but there is nothing to prevent its having been simultaneous with his keeping of a tavern and his other occupations.   As a matter of fact, he was a qualified fencing master, and an author as well.   The first entirely trustworthy information about him is concerned with his authorship; in 1570 he published a by no means brilliant ballad on the floods in Bedfordshire, etc.[2]   It is scarcely probable, however, that he himself composed this miserable song; we should think it more likely that he lent the printer his name, which, no doubt, was already celebrated by that time.   So much is certain, however, that he wrote the scenario of the play previously mentioned, *The Seven Deadly Sins*, and very likely he also composed the *Famous Victories of Henry V.*, a forerunner of Shakespeare's royal dramas about the popular "Prince Hal."   We meet with him in 1583 as one of the twelve distinguished artists from various companies, who are selected to be "The Queen's Players," and at the same time he is made groom of the chamber.   In 1587 he took the highest degree in the art of fencing as "master of the noble syence of deffence," from which we conclude that he cannot have been very old when he died.   He was probably carried off by the plague, which ravaged the country in 1588, for on a single day, the 3rd of September, he made his will, died, and was buried.[3]

---

[1] Comp. *Tarlton's Jests*, pp. 15, 21 and 26.
[2] Reprinted in *Tarlton's Jests*, pp. 126 ff.
[3] *Tarlton's Jests*, p. 12.

8—Richard Tarlton as a Clown.

From the numerous anecdotes about Tarlton we get the impression of a light-living merry fellow, who felt as much at ease when at court in the society of the Queen and the great lords—where he himself was a Lord of Mirth [1]—as when surrounded by fiddlers in a public-house. A man of quick wit, never at a loss for an answer, and sparing nobody, high or low, man or woman.

In the theatre he was the great delight of the audience from the moment when his ludicrous little body with the large head dived out from behind the back drapery. His flat nose and squinting eyes, his cap with the button, his reddish brown clown's dress, his drum and his pipe, were known to every child in London, and as soon as he stood up on tiptoe and prepared to speak, the house roared with laughter.

It was a favourite joke to challenge him to rhyme by addressing verses to him about his appearance or private circumstances. But the challengers seldom got the best of their game, for Tarlton's tongue was as sharp as it was quick. Thus it happened one day that a spectator, wishing to make game of him, asked him in tolerably good verses how he had come by his flat nose. But Tarlton was not slow, and retorted in a little improvised poem which ended thus :—

" Though my nose be flat,
My credit to save,

[1] Here within this sullen earth
Lies Dick Tarlton, lord of mirth.

(*Wits Bedlam*, 1617, quoted by Halliwell, *Tarlton's Jests*, p. 15.)

> Yet very well I can by the smell
> Scent an honest man from a knave." [1]

Altogether he was a great master in the art of improvisation, which he had no doubt studied successfully
after the Italian actors, who by this time were travelling
about England.   One of his comic scenes, which is
known to us, reminds us a good deal of the burlesques
of Scaramuccia or Arlecchino : A rich man is lying on
his death-bed, and has called his three sons to him in
order to acquaint them with his last will.   All his landed
property is left to his eldest son, who in great emotion
assures his father that he hopes he may live and enjoy
it himself.   The second son receives a large sum of
ready money to live on and to buy books with, but he
too is moved to tears and pretends that he does not
want the money, and that he trusts his good father may
live and enjoy it himself.   Now comes the last, the
prodigal son, to the death-bed.   It is Tarlton.   He
appears in a ragged and dirty shirt, a coat with only
one sleeve, stockings without heels, and a headgear of
feathers and straw.   "As to you, sirra," his father says
angrily, "you know how many times I have got you out
of Newgate and Bridewell—you have been an ungrateful
scoundrel—all I can leave you is the gallows and a
rope."   Tarlton bursts into a deluge of tears, falls on his
knees, and exclaims sobbing : "Oh, my father, that is
much more than I desire ; I hope to God that you may
live and enjoy them yourself." [2]

However, it was by his "jigs," a merry singing and

---

[1] *Tarlton's Jests*, p. 29.
[2] Halliwell-Phillipps, *Outlines*, pp. 86 ff.

dancing performance, which, according to the fashion of the time, closed the dramatic representation, that Tarlton won his greatest fame.[1] The only jig [2] which has been preserved shows us a very long humorous song, not differing in kind from our modern music-hall songs ; it is amusing and well written, and has a constantly recurring refrain, which with a small variation adapted itself to the contents of each verse. Its title is : "Tarlton's Jigge of a Horse-loade of Fooles," and the first verse runs as follows :—

> What do you lacke? what do ye lacke?
> Ive a horse loade of fooles,
> Squeaking, gibbering of everie degree ;
> Ime an excellent workeman
> And these are my tooles :
> Is not this a fine merie familie ? [3]

We can imagine Tarlton entering the stage riding on one of those ludicrous hobby-horses, which in those times were a favourite means of producing an effect, and which even now circus clowns do not disdain to use. A hobby-horse is the hollow body of a horse through which the rider sticks his legs, while a pair of artificial legs are placed astride on the animal, so that he seems

[1] The same fashion prevailed during that period in Paris, where the chansons of Gaultier Garguille enjoyed the same popular favour as Tarlton's jigs in London.

[2] It would be more correct to say, the only text of a jig, for we know the music of several of them. Compare Halliwell's *Cambridge Manuscript Rarities*, p. 8.

[3] "What do you lacke? what do you lacke?" was in those times the general cry of the seller to the customer. The jig is reprinted in the Introduction to *Tarlton's Jests* (pp. 20 ff.) after a manuscript which was in Collier's possession. It is one of the curiosities discovered by him, the authenticity of which has never been doubted.

to ride while he runs round with the body fastened to himself.   In front of him he probably had a basket full of dolls representing fools, which he offered for sale while singing his song.

The first he presents is himself; his name is Dick, he is a fool-actor, whose portrait hangs on every wall, so that nobody can mistake the likeness.   Moreover, he has his father's "lovelie visnomie," his two eyes and flat nose, and "he comes of a rare witty family."

Next, he presents a Puritan fool, whom he calls "Goose-son," *i.e.* Stephen Gosson, one of the most zealous antagonists of actors, whose "School of Abuse" we have mentioned before.   He is very badly treated as a common hypocrite "of a very numerous family."

Then comes the "fool of state," who is born very small, but "would fain be very great"; "of a very ancient family"; and the poet who drinks sack and canary in "The Hat" or "The Rose," "of a rare wine-bibing family"; the doctor who kills us with such skill and art that he makes dying quite a pleasure; "of a marvellously learned family"; the lover-fool who sings to his lute about his lost luck; "of a most melancholy family"; the alderman who hates all kinds of wisdom, but most of all in plays; "of a very obstinate family"; and the country fool, who comes to town to be made a gentleman, though he is but a "rustic clown"; "of a Somersetshire family."

Of course, Tarlton, who performed this jig on the stage of "The Curtain," knew how to characterise each of these different types by their special gestures and the peculiarities of class, which in the old time much more than nowadays distinguished people from each other.

Tarlton became the principal exponent of the genuine unadulterated English humour, untainted with the bigoted Puritan moroseness, and unawed by the overweening pride of the court and nobility, the two powers which have always done their best to crush healthy national mirth. Tarlton even occupied a peculiar position at court. Without being in any way a court-fool like the famous William Sommer of Henry VIII., he was allowed the privilege of free speech to the Queen, which nobody else possessed. Fuller relates:[1] "Our Tarlton was master of his faculty. When Queen Elizabeth was serious, I dare not say sullen, and out of good humour, he could *undumpish* her at his pleasure. Her highest favourites would, in some cases, go to Tarlton before they would go to the Queen, and he was their usher to prepare their advantageous access unto her. In a word, he told the Queen more of her faults than most of her chaplains, and cured her melancholy better than all of her physicians.

"Much of his merriment lay in his very looks and actions, according to the epitaph written upon him:—

" Hic situs est cujus poterat vox, actio, vultus,
　　Ex Heraclito reddere Democritum.

" Indeed, the same words, spoken by another, would hardly move a merry man to smile, which, uttered by him, would force a sad soul to laughter."

We have reason to question whether he stood in

---

[1] Fuller's *Worthies*, ed. 1662, p. 47 (Staffordshire).

any intimate relation with the new time and its new-born
dramatic literature.   He was probably not an actor in
the modern sense of the word, an exponent of human
character, such as the time immediately after him was
to produce, and though he performed "parts" in various
plays,[1] he always remained the same Tarlton.

However, such as he was, he not only gained
immense popularity, but he created a school, though
his pupils never equalled their master.   He was surrounded by a staff of comic actors like Knell, Bentley,
Mils, Wilson, Crosse and Lanam,[2] among whom Knell,
as we see from the preceding note, was the original
Prince Henry in the ante-Shakespearean *Henry V.*,
while Robert Wilson was one of the companions of
James Burbage and a popular dramatic author, of whom
we have spoken before.   They are all mentioned by
their later colleague, Thomas Heywood, in company

---

[1] In *Tarlton's Jests* (pp. 24 ff.) we read the following rather amusing little
anecdote, which at least shows that he was capable of playing other parts
than his usual clown : "At the Bull at Bishopsgate was a play of Henry the
fift, wherein the judge was to take a box on the eare ; and because he was
absent that should take the blow, Tarlton himselfe ever forward to please,
tooke upon him to play the same judge, besides his owne part of the clown ;
and Knell then playing Henry the fift, hit Tarlton a sound boxe indeed,
which made the people laugh the more because it was he, but anon the
judge goes in, and immediately Tarlton in his clownes cloathes comes out
and askes the actors what newes ; O, saith one, hadst thou been here thou
shouldest have seen Prince Henry hit the judge a terrible box on the eare :
What, man, said Tarlton, strike a judge?   It is true, y faith, said the other.
No other like, said Tarlton, and it could not be but terrible to the judge,
when the report so terrifies me, that me thinkes the blow remains still on
my cheeke, that it burnes againe.   The people laughed at this mightily :
and to this day I have heard it commended for rare ; but no marvell, for he
had many of these.   But I would see our clowns in these dayes do the like :
no, I warrant ye, and yet they thinke well of themselves to."

[2] They are mentioned in this order by Thomas Heywood, as a school of
actors which he had never seen himself.—*Apology for Actors*, p. 43.

with "all these Doctors, Zannis, Pantaloons and Harlequins, in which the French, and especially the Italians,
have distinguished themselves," and this fact confirms
our supposition that this first period was influenced by
the *Commedia dell' Arte.*

To a somewhat later generation belonged artists like
William Kemp, Robert Arnim, Gabriel Spencer, Thomas
Pope, Augustine Phillips and William Sly, the first of
whom, Kemp, undoubtedly gained the greatest celebrity.
He really became Tarlton's inheritor, as Heywood says,
"of Her Majesty's favour as well as of the good opinion
and thoughts of the public in general." But it may be
doubted if he equalled his predecessor in naïve and
brilliant comic power.

It seems to me that the small amount of information
we possess about Kemp gives the impression of a
business-like, swaggering, coarse artist, while Tarlton
was a born comic genius. Where Kemp is mentioned
in the literature of the time, allusions are made to his
ignorance and lack of culture side by side with his
great popularity. Thus, especially in a previously
quoted scene from the University play, *The Return from
Parnassus*, in which he appears together with Richard
Burbage, and speaks about "that writer Ovid and that
writer Metamorphosis." [1] While in the whole of this
scene Burbage is represented as a well-bred and educated
man, we get an image of Kemp as a rough, swaggering
juggler. He cannot distinguish the names of the two
students Philomusus and Studioso, but calls them "Mr
Phil and Mr Otioso"; he boasts of his fame and says

[1] Compare above, p. 43.

to the students : . . . "for honours, who of more report than Dick Burbage and Will Kemp? he is not counted a gentleman that knowes not Dick Burbage and Will Kemp; there is not a country wench that can dance Sellenger's Round but can talk of Dick Burbage and Will Kemp"; whereupon Philomusus adds: "Indeed, M. Kemp, you are very famous."

The only literary work left by Kemp also shows his vanity and self-complacency. It is a short description of his celebrated Morris-dance from London to Norwich, one of those eccentric journeys of which Englishmen were so fond in those days. What Kemp pledged himself to do was this; in nine days he was to dance the whole way from London to Norwich, of course not un-interruptedly, but without walking or driving at all, only moving in the steps of the Morris-dance, for which he was particularly noted.[1] The Morris was a kind of rustic dance accompanied by the jingling of bells which were fastened to the dancer's legs, and by the sounds of a drum and a pipe played by a musician. The drawing on the title-page of his little book[2] shows us Kemp dancing along the road, accompanied by his drummer, Thomas Sly (perhaps a relative of William Sly, the comic actor), and by his servant and an umpire, who had to see that the dance was properly executed.

[1] He styles himself "Cavaliero Kemp, head-master of Morris-dancers" (Kemp's *Nine Daies Wonder*, p. 3).

[2] Its title is: *Kemp's Nine Daies Wonder. Performed in a daunce from London to Norwich. Containing the pleasure, paines, and kinde entertain-ment of William Kemp between London and that Citty in his late Morrice.* London, 1600. This exceedingly rare book has been reprinted by A. Dyce for the Camden Society.

9—William Kemp Dancing a Morris Dance.

On the first Monday in Lent, 1599, in the early morning, he danced out of London while his drummer played merrily, and old and young followed him on the way, throwing sixpences and coppers to him and crying many a "good speed on the journey." The dance went into the country, where the populace crowded curiously round him, and everyone wanted him to pass through their particular village; where nut-brown country-lassies would borrow jingles of him and dance with him on the road; where he stopped in the inns and had great difficulty in refusing the number of brimming cups which were offered him by gay millers and enthusiastic smiths; where he sometimes danced in water and mud up to his knees without giving up the task; at other times in beautiful clear dry moonlight nights, till at last he reached Norwich, where the whole populace were assembled to receive him. He brought his dance to an end with a smart jump over the church wall, after which he wound up with a grand festival at the house of the Mayor of Norwich, who, moreover, made him a present of £5.

In a lively and not unamiable way Kemp describes the experiences of each day in his little book, which gives us a pretty clear idea of the man, an actor of Shakespeare, who, like an organ-grinder, accepts the coppers of the peasants on the road, and nevertheless is seated side by side with the mayor and aldermen, knights and ladies, who honour him for his athletic feat; a vain, penny-loving, yet tolerably attractive and clever juggler, who one day acts in one of Shakespeare's finest plays, dances in a country inn the next, and on the third

is admitted perhaps to Her Majesty's table.   The man
is a type of a certain kind of Renaissance actor.

Of Kemp's theatrical career we know a little more
than of Tarlton's, but not very much.

Curiously enough, the first entirely trustworthy information about Kemp's stage-work dates from Denmark.
It is a well-known fact that from the close of the sixteenth
and quite to the middle of the seventeenth century
English companies travelled through Germany, Austria,
France, the Netherlands, Sweden and Denmark.   They
were very successful everywhere, both with the courts
and among the people ; chiefly, it is probable, with their
dancing and playing, though in Germany they also
performed their usual dramatic répertoire and were
gradually naturalised.[1]

Denmark was one of the first countries to be visited
by these companies.   As early as in 1579 Frederick II.
engaged a company of "instrumentalists" at his court,
under the management of an Italian named Zoëga.
Besides the Italian leader, the company included both
German and English members,[2] of whom the English
were much better remunerated than the Germans.

In 1586 a company of much greater importance
arrived at Elsinore, where the King frequently held his

---

[1] In later years the study of the travels and work of these companies has
made considerable progress, especially since the publication in 1865 of the
pioneer book by Albert Cohn, *Shakespeare in Germany*.   Throughout the
annual issues of the *Shakespeare Jahrbuch* we find numerous interesting
essays and notes, some by Cohn himself, some by Johannes Bolte and
Johannes Meissner.

[2] Among them was the unfortunate Thomas Bull, whose love story and
beheading have been described by Dr Ad. Hansen after the municipal
records of Elsinore in *Tilskueren* of July 1900.

court. It included such noted members as William Kemp, Thomas Pope and George Bryan, all of them well-known clowns, who figure in the list of principal actors in the plays of Shakespeare published in the folio edition of 1623. The little company consisted of five members besides Kemp and his " boy," Daniel Jones. Kemp seems to have belonged to the company as a kind of distinguished guest. He only remained two months in Denmark, and received a larger amount of board-money than the others. In the accounts of the court the entry concerning Kemp runs as follows: "William Kempe, instrumentist, received in board-money for two months for himself and a boy named Daniell Jones, which he had earned from the 17th of June, when he entered the service, and moreover for one month, which was given him at his departure, together three months, each month 12 Dalers . . . xxxvi Dalers."

The English guests probably all belonged to " Lord Leicester's Men," consequently to the company of the Burbages, and most likely came direct from London with a large embassy, which Frederick II. had sent to Queen Elizabeth in April, and which must have arrived at Elsinore at the date when the company was engaged (June 17th). At the beginning of the year Kemp, and perhaps the others also, had been in Utrecht with their protector, Lord Leicester himself, who was staying in the Netherlands to fan the revolt against Philip II. ; but in the meantime he had been back in England. This appears from a passage in a letter from Philip Sidney, a nephew of Leicester's, to Walsingham, his father-in-law, in which he says that at an earlier date he had sent a message home with Will, "Mylord of Leicester's jesting plaier." [1]

Will Kemp now returned to England, while his travelling companions remained some time in Denmark, and then were engaged by the Elector of Saxony. Most likely he joined his old company again, and acted with them at " The Theatre "[2] during the following years. We know for certain that he played Peter in *Romeo and Juliet* here, for in the oldest editions of this piece (the quartos of 1599 and 1609) his name has crept in instead of the name of the part, so that (in act iv., scene 5) we read : " enter William Kemp " instead of "enter Peter." We do not know any of his other parts on this stage, but as he is specially mentioned as a principal actor in Shakespeare's plays, and as he was undoubtedly a great celebrity as a comic actor, it is probable that during this period he acted such parts as Bottom in *A Midsummer Night's Dream*; Lance in *The Two Gentlemen of Verona*, which seems to be written for his special capacity ; Costard in *Love's Labour Lost* ; one of the Dromios in *A Comedy of Errors*, etc.

When " The Theatre " was pulled down in 1598, he went with his company to " The Curtain," and there played Dogberry in *Much Ado About Nothing* ; for this we possess the same kind of evidence as for his impersonation of Peter. At " The Curtain," moreover, he

[1] Albert Cohn (and others after him) is of opinion that Kemp and the rest of the company travelled direct from the Netherlands to Denmark. But though those times were not accustomed to quick postal communication, we must say that it would have been absurd for anybody to send a letter home to England by a man who went to Denmark.

[2] Not at "The Blackfriars," which was not built till 1596, and Kemp is not likely to have ever acted there.

played one of the principal parts in Ben Jonson's *Every Man in His Humour*; which it was, we do not know, but I feel inclined to think that it was Brainworm.

However, during this whole period—from his return from Denmark in 1586 to 1598—he did not stay uninterruptedly at the theatres of the Burbages. At any rate, from the 19th of February to the 22nd of June 1592, a part of "Lord Leicester's" company, which since 1588 had been "Lord Strange's," played under Henslowe and Alleyn, and probably at "The Newington."[1] That Kemp was included in the cast here we know for certain, from the fact that on the 10th or 11th of June 1592[2] a new anonymous play was performed for the first time; its title was: *A Knack to Know a Knave, with Kemp's Applauded Merriments*. The piece is still extant, and Kemp's *Applauded Merriments* prove to be a perfectly senseless and spiritless little interlude, performed by artisans.[3] It is to be supposed, however, that Kemp improvised the jokes which created the success of the play, for, like Tarlton's, his strong point was improvisation. At any rate, this piece proves unmistakably that in 1592 Kemp played under Alleyn and Henslowe, for on the title-page of its first edition (1594) we read : "as it has been acted several times by Edw. Allen and his company." He had not, however, left his own company, "Lord Strange's Men," as Collier[4] thinks, but, for what

---

[1] Not, as asserted by Fleay (*English Drama*, ii. p. 310), at "The Rose," the building of which was not completed at this time.

[2] Comp. Henslowe's *Diary*, p. 28.

[3] It is reprinted in Dyce's edition of *A Nine Daies Wonder*, pp. xxiii. ff.

[4] *English Dramatic Poetry*, iii. 335, where Collier indeed speaks of "The Lord Chamberlain's Company," which did not exist at all in 1592, when its name was " Lord Strange's Men."

reason, is unknown, this company had for a time sub-
mitted to the leadership of Henslowe and Alleyn.   This
fact appears distinctly from the headlines of Henslowe's
accounts for this season, which run : " In God's name,
Amen, 1591[2],[1] beginning the 19th of February, my Lord
Strange's men, as follows." Till February 1593 Kemp
and his companions probably remained under Henslowe
and Alleyn. *A Knack to Know a Knave* was performed
for the last time on January 25th, 1593,[2] whereafter,
very likely, they again returned to the Burbages.

Later, however, matters came to a decisive rupture
between Kemp and the company, or rather, if we dare
venture on the wild paths of conjecture, between Kemp
and Shakespeare.   We can scarcely imagine a greater
contrast than these two men.   Shakespeare, noble and
reticent, quietly writes one masterpiece after another, but
never about himself, never about his own greatness,
never against his colleagues ; unnoticed, even without
noticing it himself, he becomes the greatest man of his
time.   Kemp, noisy and coarse, fills England and the
Continent with the tinkling of his clown's bells, his
pipes and drums ; advertises himself without shame and
without measure, and becomes the common topic much
more than Shakespeare, which naturally gives him the
idea that he himself is a far greater man than the other.

These two are fellow-actors.   They play together
daily and in the same pieces, which, moreover, are
written by Shakespeare himself, and the representation

[1] Henslowe frequently mixes up the Old and the New Style in his dates.
In the middle of this year of his accounts he suddenly passes from 1591
to 1592.
[2] Henslowe's *Diary*, p. 30.

of which is conducted by him. A rupture between them was inevitable. From his tours on the Continent, and from such more or less mediocre performances as his above-mentioned "*Applauded Merriments*," Kemp had fallen into habits of improvisation, and of taking possession of the stage, which Shakespeare did not like, and from which he considered it his duty to purge the theatre. That down to a much later period Kemp was famed, or ill-famed, for his heedless running after witticisms, we gather from *The Antipodes*, a piece by Brome, in which there is a scene between the nobleman, Letoy, and an actor, Byplay. Letoy endeavours to make the actor see that it is not right to add anything to the part, or to have direct intercourse with the public, but that actors have to follow the course of the dialogue, and pay attention to what is going on on the stage. Byplay excuses himself in the following lines :—

> " That is a way, my lord, has been allowed
> On elder stages, to move mirth and laughter."

But Letoy answers :—

> " Yes, in the days of Tarleton and Kemp,
> Before the stage was purg'd from barbarism,
> And brought to the perfection it now shines with :
> Then fools and jesters spent their wits, because
> The poets were wise enough to save their own
> For profitabler uses."

Now, we cannot justly say that Shakespeare spared his wit in his comic characters, but probably he did not like his actors, any more than other authors, and with greater right than any of them, to treat the public to the jokes which occurred to them at the moment, instead of offering those which he himself had taken the trouble of providing with wit and point; especially if these jokes, as we may suspect of those delivered by Kemp, were coarse, and not in keeping with Shakespeare's own taste.   In Kemp and Shakespeare, then, we meet not only with a conflict between two men, but with a collision between two kinds of taste, two types within the domain of dramatic art.

Shakespeare did not fail to be explicit in expressing his opinion about actors of the kind to which he thought Kemp belonged.   In the rules for the players which he has put into the mouth of Hamlet, he uses the following sharp words, which are applicable to all times :[1] " Let those that play your clowns speak no more than is set down for them ; for there be of them that will themselves laugh, to set on some quantity of barren spectators to laugh too ; though, in the meantime, some necessary question of the play be then to be considered : that's villainous, and shews a most pitiful ambition in the fool that uses it."

That these words were aimed directly at Kemp is very probable, though, of course, it cannot be proved.   About this time Kemp had left the Burbage company.   Doubtless he did not go to " The Globe " at all, when this theatre was opened in 1599.   For, while he is put down as one of the cast of Jonson's *Every Man in his Humour* in 1598, he is not mentioned among the actors of *Every Man Out of his Humour* by the same author, which

[1] *Hamlet*, iii. 2.

was performed at "The Globe" in 1599. It was in this year that he undertook his famous Morris-dance to Norwich, and perhaps he afterwards made other journeys to the Continent. In the above-mentioned scene in *The Return from Parnassus*, which dates from about 1601, Kemp is greeted as having recently arrived from abroad. Philomusus says to him : "What, Mr Kemp, how doth the Emperor of Germany ? " and Studioso : " Welcome, Mr Kemp, from dancing the morrice over the Alpes."

After his rupture with Burbage and Shakespeare, Kemp very likely spent a year on the Continent. In a play called *The Travels of the Three English Brothers*, he is represented as staying in Venice, where he is having a burlesque and not very decent conversation with an Italian comrade, "Signior Harlakin" and his wife. However, we do not possess any positive evidence of his having visited either Germany or Italy. His name is not found included in the various companies which travelled in Germany at this period.

In 1602, in any case, he is again in London, acting under Henslowe and Alleyn as one of "the Earl of Worcester's Men." We gather from Henslowe's *Diary* that on the 10th of March 1602 he borrows "in Redy monye twentye shillenges for his necessary usses." [1] . . .

The later part of his life is enveloped in obscurity. It does not seem probable, in spite of Collier's assertion, that he returned to Burbage's company. However, the document on which Collier founds his belief—a complaint of the Lord Mayor in 1605 against Kemp, Arnim

---

[1] Henslowe's *Diary*, pp. 215, 237, 238.

and other players of " The Blackfriars "[1]—is evidently a forgery, and even if it could be proved that Kemp had played at " The Blackfriars " in 1605, it does not follow that he had returned to Burbage's company, for, as we have proved above, it was not till 1608 that the King's men acted at " The Blackfriars."

The year of Kemp's death is unknown, as is that of his birth.   I think it probable, however, that he was still alive in 1607, when *The Three English Brothers* was acted ; in the scene where he appears under his own name there is nothing to prove that a dead man is represented.   It is even probable that he impersonated himself in the play ; in that case he belonged at the time to " The Queen's Men."

Kemp is not likely to have left other literary works besides his little *Nine Daies Wonder*.   A number of jigs indeed bear his name, but doubtless they were not composed, only performed by him.[2]

II

The Tragedians—" King Cambyses' Vein " and Shakespeare's Opinion About It—Edward Alleyn as an Artist and as a Man.

THE custom of improvisation in comic dramatic art, though it did not die with Kemp, certainly went out of fashion after his death.   If it had ever had a footing in tragedy, it had long been abolished.

[1] Collier, *English Dramatic Poetry*, iii. 352.

[2] A pamphlet directed against the Puritans and published under the name of W. Kemp has led Collier and others to believe that our clown took part in the literary struggle against the Puritans.   This strange error rests on the mistake of confusing Kemp the actor with a schoolmaster and pedagogue in Plymouth, who bore the same name.

Nevertheless, we can trace an old and a new style in tragic acting also. The serious performers of the Middle Ages were mostly artisans and petty tradesmen, and it was probably from these classes that the first generation of professional tragedians was recruited. The first builder of theatres in London, the actor James Burbage, was a joiner by profession; the second great theatrical manager, Philip Henslowe, was a dyer. Among the earlier performers of the pre-Shakespearean sanguinary répertoire of tragedies, no doubt there was many a master-weaver Bottom, carpenter Quince and tailor Starveling. To semi-amateurs nothing is more welcome than the external display of violence on which these pieces were based, where roaring and shouting cover the lack of capacity for emotional speech, where rolling of the eyes replaces well developed facial play, and violent, purposeless movements are substituted for expressive gestures.

Let us hear what Bottom says (*Midsummer Night's Dream*, Act i., sc. 2): " . . . I could play Ercles rarely, or a part to tear a cat in, to make all split.

> " The raging rocks,
> With shivering shocks,
> Shall break the locks
> Of prison gates :
> And Phibbus' car
> Shall shine from far,
> And make and mar
> The foolish fates."

" This was lofty ! . . . This is Ercles' vein, a tyrant's vein, a lover is more condoling."

This style was particularly odious to Shakespeare. In *Henry IV.* he calls it "King Cambyses' vein," a splendid expression, which ought to serve for ever as a description of this sort of art. It is put into the mouth of old John Falstaff, who, in the famous public-house scene in the second act, is about to represent the father of Prince Henry in this style :—

"Give me a cup of sack to make mine eyes look red, that it may be thought I have wept, for I must speak in passion, and I will do it in King Cambyses' vein."[1]

"A lamentable tragedy mixed ful of pleasant mirth contegning the life of Cambises" was an old play by Thomas Preston, written ab. 1561, published in 1570, in which ghastly horrors are mixed up with burlesque scenes in the old-fashioned way. But the style of this play in itself has not the slightest resemblance to that of Falstaff in the speech he makes to the prince—it might rather be called a little euphuistic—so it cannot be the style of writing, but the manner of acting which Shakespeare means to parody, the "tyrant vein," the old-fashioned exaggerated grandiloquence, which he detested and against which he struggled in every way, though he did not conquer it. It still flourishes and will go on flourishing as long as there are actors without talent to use it as the best screen for their incapacity. This style indeed affords the great advantage to the performer of gaining quite as much admiration from the ordinary public as true and genuine art. That is why Mrs Quickly, the hostess of the Boar's Head Tavern, falls into ecstasies at the first verses recited by Falstaff.

[1] *Henry IV.*, Part I., ii. 4.

Hostess : " O, the Father, how he holds his coun-
            tenance ! "
Falstaff : " For God's sake, lords, convey my trustful
            queen,
            For tears do stop the flood-gates of her
            eyes."
Hostess : " O rare! he doth it as like one of these
            harlotry players as I ever see."

Elsewhere (in *Richard III.*)[1] Shakespeare describes
the manners of a villain on the stage.   It is in the scene
where Gloster incites Buckingham to deceive the Lord
Mayor.   Buckingham gives the somewhat conceited
reply :—

" Tut, I can counterfeit the deep tragedian ;
   Speak, and look back, and pry on every side,
   Tremble and start at wagging of a straw,
   Intending deep suspicion : ghostly looks
   Are at my service, like enforced smiles ;
   And both are ready in their offices,
   At any time, to grace my stratagem."

Naturally this exaggerated manner was repugnant to
the refined and self-controlled mind of Shakespeare.   He
evidently burned to express his disgust of it.   As a rule,
he keeps his own personality in the background, and
scarcely ever expresses his private opinion in literary or
artistic controversies ; but for once he speaks his mind
and deals a blow at his antagonists in art, which is much
harder, much more serious, and more directly personal in

[1] Act iii. Sc. 5.

aim than any of the allusions mentioned above. The attack is found in *Hamlet*, which, on the whole, contains more personal and actual self-expression than any other of Shakespeare's plays ; but which, it must be added, appeared at a time when the tide in theatrical controversy ran high.

The old idea in *Hamlet*, which was not Shakespeare's own, of making the king betray himself by acting before him a play in which his own crime was represented, afforded Shakespeare an opportunity of revealing his own artistic creed in an unusually outspoken way, and of doing it in a form so personal and concise, that it ought to be the *vade mecum* of every true actor :—

Hamlet : "Speak the speech, I pray you, as I pronounced it to you, trippingly on the tongue : but if you mouth it, as many of your players do, I had as lief the town-crier spoke my lines. Nor do saw the air too much with your hand, thus, but use all gently ; for in the very torrent, tempest, and, as I may say, the whirlwind of passion, you must acquire and beget a temperance that may give it smoothness. O, it offends me to the soul to hear a robustious periwig-pated fellow tear a passion to tatters, to very rags, to split the ears of the groundlings, who for the most part are capable of nothing but inexplicable dumb-shows and noise : I would have such a fellow whipped for o'erdoing Termagant ; it outherods Herod. . . . O, there be players that I have seen play, and heard others praise, and that highly, not to speak it profanely, that neither having the accent of Christians nor the gait of Christian, pagan nor man, have so strutted and bellowed that I have thought some

10—William Shakespeare (the Droeshont-Flowers portrait).

of nature's journeymen had made men and not made them well, they imitated humanity so abominably."

To this the actor to whom the speech is addressed replies : " I hope we have reformed that indifferently with us, sir."

But Hamlet (Shakespeare) continues inexorably : "O, reform it altogether." And thereupon he delivers the little side-blow at Kemp which we quoted before.

Now the play which is subsequently acted does not offer any opportunity for particular admonitions of this kind ; there is no fool and no "tyrant" who might have an occasion for displaying his bad points in acting. Evidently this little lecture has an aim which lies outside the subject of the play. It is an attack on a school of acting which was distasteful to Shakespeare. And what kind of school it was does not seem difficult to guess, especially if one passage of Hamlet's speech is rightly understood.

Shakespeare says : " I would have such a fellow whipped for o'erdoing Termagant ; it out-herods Herod." Now, as all commentators on Shakespeare know, Termagant and Herod are two characters frequently appearing in the Mysteries of the Middle Ages. Termagant, originally a deity supposed to be worshipped by the Saracens, stood afterwards in general for an exotic knave and tyrant. This name we meet everywhere in ancient heroic fiction in slightly varying forms, such as Tervagant, Termagaunt, Terrogant, Tarmagant. Herod is the villain and tyrant in the Passion Plays properly so-called.

Now it seems somewhat strange that Shakespeare

should point to mediæval types as examples of bad acting ;
but a circumstance to which the commentators have paid
no attention is this : these two characters undoubtedly
belonged to the répertoire of Edward Alleyn.   In Henslowe's *Diary* frequent mention is made of a play, the
scenario of which we know, and which bears the title of
Tamar Cam or *Tambercam*.[1] Considering Henslowe's
usual extraordinary way of spelling, it would not be
surprising if these names were meant for *Termagant*.
That the subject of this play was " Mahometan," *i.e.*
heathen and foreign, we see from the scenario,[2] in which
the King, or the "Shaugh'en,"[3] of Persia makes his appearance.   Moreover, there is an abundance of ghosts and
other supernatural beings in the piece, which agrees
perfectly well with *Termagant*.   And further, Alleyn is
unmistakably indicated in the scenario as having played
the title part. He also owned the play, as in 1602
Henslowe buys the book of him for £2.[4] It seems to
have been popular and widely known ; for ten years,
from 1592 to 1602, it is on the répertoire (of course, with
interruptions), and it is probable that it had been revived
at the time when *Hamlet* was performed.   So, if Shakespeare says that he " would have such a fellow whipped
for [even] o'erdoing Termagant," I have not the slightest
doubt that these words, clear enough to all spectators,
were meant as a hit at his rival, Alleyn.

As to *Herod*, there has been no evidence hitherto to

---

[1] Also *Tamour Cam* and *Tamber Came*.
[2] Reprinted in Malone : *Historical Account*, Plate ii.
[3] In seventeenth century writers it is sometimes spelt "Shawne."
[4] Henslowe's *Diary*, pp. 227 and 241.

prove that a play with this title was acted under Alleyn in the period previous to *Hamlet*. Much later, about 1622, we know that a play by Markham and William Sampson was acted at " The Red Bull," the title of which was *Herod and Antipater with the death of Fair Marian*.[1] Though Henslowe's *Diary* does not contain any direct information about a play with this title and this subject, it may be proved, nevertheless, that such a play really was included in Alleyn's répertoire even shortly before the representation of *Hamlet*, as in Henslowe's *Diary*, in an inventory of apparel of 1598,[2] belonging to " The Lord Admiral's Men," *i.e.* Alleyn's company, I find the following entry : " Item iiii. Herevodes cottes and iii sogers [soldiers] cottes and i green gown for Maryan."

Now, if such a play was acted by " The Lord Admiral's Men," it may be taken for granted that Alleyn played the part of Herod, as all such violent characters belonged to his province. So the words, "he out-herods Herod," are another allusion to the exaggerated acting of Alleyn and his school.

In speaking, as we did above, of an old and a new school, of course we must not be understood to imply that Alleyn and Shakespeare represented two genera-tions, of which Shakespeare belonged to the younger ; for the two antagonists were of almost the same age, Alleyn being even the younger of the two. But a young person may very well adhere to an old school, be

[1] Comp. Fr. G. Fleay, *English Drama*, ii. 175.
[2] This inventory, the MS. of which no longer exists, is reprinted in Malone's *Additions*, pp. 375 ff.

supported by it, and refuse to adopt the progress which is the result of a more refined taste and greater artistic intelligence.

And this, we suppose, was the case with Edward Alleyn. He was two years younger than Shakespeare, being born on September 1st, 1566, but he was probably brought up from his childhood for the stage,[1] and he obtained celebrity at a marvellously early age, considering the branch in which he acted. His father was a publican and porter to the Queen, and died leaving a considerable fortune, when his son Edward was only four years old. His wife afterwards married a shop-keeper of the name of Brown, who has been erroneously identified with the actor, Robert Brown,[2] especially known for his professional journeys on the Continent. Mrs Alleyn's second husband was a John Brown, who had nothing to do with the theatre.

In 1586, when Alleyn was twenty years old, we find him mentioned for the first time as one of " The Earl of Worcester's Players," and in the following year he is already acting a part of such importance as Tamburlaine the Great in Marlowe's play of that name. The two following years bring him the gigantic tasks of Dr Faustus, and of Barrabas in *The Jew of Malta*, both also by Marlowe, as well as the title-part of Robert

[1] According to Fuller in his *Worthies* (ii. 84, ed. 1811), and there is no reason to doubt it, as it is perfectly in accordance with Alleyn's earlier career that he should have played female parts as a boy, and, as Fuller has it, been "bred a stage player."

[2] Albert Cohn makes this mistake on the authority of Collier's assertion that the shopkeeper and the actor Brown were the same person. Comp. Collier's *Memoirs of Alleyn*, p. iii., and Cohn's *Shakespeare in Germany*, p. xxxi.

The Tragicall History
of the Life and Death
of *Doctor Faustus.*

Written by *Ch.* *Mar*

LONDON,
Printed for *Iohn Wright,* and are to be fold at his fhop
Without Newgate, at the fi.. .. .: .he
Bi!   1636.

11—Alleyn as Dr Faustus.

Greene's *Orlando Furioso.*[1]   It is almost incomprehensible that a young man of little more than twenty
years should have been able to assume and represent
these indescribably violent and, to a certain extent, really
powerful characters, which at the same time differ very
much from each other.   He must have won his fame at
a stroke, but probably he at once adopted a manner
which became fatal to his later artistic career.   At
scarcely twenty-six years of age, he is mentioned as the
leading tragedian in England, and even in the same
breath with the comic stars of the elder generation,
Tarlton, Knell and Bentley.   In his *Pierce Penniless's
Supplication to the Devil*, which appeared in 1592,
Thomas Nash draws a comparison between English and
foreign actors, which is interesting in itself, and which
in an unmistakable way shows Alleyn's celebrity at the
time.   He writes : " Our players [2] are not as the players
beyond the sea, a sort of squirting baudie comedians,
that haue whores and common curtizans to play womens
parts, and forbeare no immodest speach or unchast
action that may procure laughter ; but our sceane is
more stately furnisht than euen it was in the time of
Roscius, our representations honorable, and full of gallaunt
resolution, not consisting like theirs of a pantaloun,
a whore and a zanie, but of emperours, kings and princes,

[1] The MS. of his part in this last play, in Alleyn's own hand, is preserved
in Dulwich College as a rare relic.   It is the only extant part belonging to
the Shakespearean period, and it shows that the parts were written out in
the same way as nowadays, but with very short cues.   The whole part is
reprinted in *Memoirs of Alleyn*, Appendix, pp. 198-213.

[2] The original has *playes*, but this is evidently a misprint, especially as
we read in a marginal note : " A comparison of our players and the players
beyond the sea."

whose true tragedies (Sophocleo cothurno) they doo vaunt.

"Not Roscius nor Esope, those tragedians admired before Christ was borne, could euer performe more in action than famous Ned Alleyn. I must accuse our poets of sloth and partialitie, that they will not boast in large impressions what worthie men (above all nations) England affoords. Other countreyes cannot haue a fidler breake a string but they will put it in print, . . . if I euer write any thing in Latine (as I hope one day I shall), not a man of any desert heere amongst us, but I will haue up. Tarlton, Ned Alleyn, Knell, Bentley, shall be made knowen to Fraunce, Spayne and Italie; and not a part that they surmounted in more than other but I will there note and set downe, with the manner of their habites and attyre."

Unfortunately this hope of Nash's was never realised ; neither in Latin nor in English did he describe these actors, which we regret very much, as we should have liked to know something about their way of acting. The two pictures reproduced here of two of Alleyn's parts, Faustus and Hieronymo in Kyd's *Spanish Tragedy*, give us little information ; in the first place because they are very inferior in themselves, and in the second, because it is not ascertained that they represent Alleyn, though it is quite probable that the unskilled draughtsman took his subjects from the traditional representations.

So much is certain, that his reputation as an actor did not make Alleyn forget his love of business, which was probably his ruling passion. In his twenty-first year he is in partnership both with his elder brother,

12 —Alleyn as Hieronimo.

John, who, like his father, was a publican, but who also occupied himself with stage matters; and also with the noted travelling actors and managers, Robert Browne and Richard Jones, in a business for the sale of "play-books" (*i.e.* manuscripts of plays), costumes, and musical instruments—Richard Jones, however, whom we know from his letter quoted above, in which he requests a loan of his well-to-do colleague, in January 1588 sold his share to Edward Alleyn for £30, 10s.[1] Four years later Alleyn appears for a time as leader of "Lord Strange's Company," but in the following year (1593) the plague was raging violently, and all acting was prohibited in London; so he set out on a tour in the provinces with his company.

Six months previously he had married Joan Wood-ward, the step-daughter of Philip Henslowe, of whom he was evidently fond, and whom he treated well. While the plague was ravaging London, and Alleyn was travelling in the provinces with his companions, the newly married couple exchanged a number of letters, some of which have been found at Dulwich College, which give us an amusing picture of the man, if not of the actor, Alleyn. He appears as a home-loving, careful, practical and affectionate man, whose thoughts are shared equally between his little "mouse," as he calls his wife, his woollen stockings, his spinach and his horses, but who has not a word to spare for his art, and is most unlike our idea of an actor, whose particular task it was to represent the wildest and

---

[1] This we learn from a contract between Alleyn and Jones, printed in an Appendix to Collier's *Memoirs of Alleyn*, p. 198.

most insanely bloodthirsty characters ever produced in
literature.   He writes, for instance, on the first of
August from Bristol :—

"This be delyvered to mr. hinslo, on of the gromes
of his maist. chamber ; dwelling on the bank sid, right
over against the clink.

"My good sweete mouse, I comend me hartely to
you And to my father, my mother and my sister bess,
hopinge in God, though the sicknes be round about you,
yett by his mercy itt may escape your house, which by
the grace of God it shall.   therefore use this corse :—
kepe your house fayr and clean, which I knowe you will,
and every evening throwe water before your dore and in
your bake sid, and have in your windows good store of
reue and herbe of grace, and with all the grace of God,
which must be obteynd by prayers ; and so doinge, no
doubt but the Lord will mercifully defend you.   now,
good mouse, I have no newse to send you but this, thatt
we have all our helth, for which the Lord be praysed.
I reseved your Letter at Bristo by richard canly, for the
which I thank you.   I have sent you by this berer,
Thomas popes kinsman, my whit wascote, because it is
a trobell to me to cary it.   reseve it with this letter,
And lay it up for me till I com.   if you send any
more Letters, send to me by the cariers of Shrowsbury,
or to Westchester, or to York, to be kept till my Lord
Strange's players com. and thus, sweett hart, with my
harty comenda. to all our frends, I sett from Bristo this
Wensday after Saynt James his day, being redy to begin
the playe of hary of cornwall. mouse, do my harty

commend. to Mr. grigs, his wife, and all his houshold, and to my sister phillyps.

"Your Loving housband

" E. ALLEYN.

" Mouse, you send me no newes of any things; you should send of your domestycall matters, such things as hapens att home; as how your distilled watter proves, or this or that, or any thing, what you will.

"And, Jug, I pray you, lett my orayng tawny stokins of wolen be dyed a very good blak against I com hom, to wear in the winter. you sente me nott word of my garden, but next tym you will; but remember this in any case, that all that bed which was parsley in the month of September you sowe it with spinage, for then is the tym. I would do it my selfe, but we shall nott com hom till allholland tyd. and so, swett mous, farwell, and broke our Long Jorney with patience."

This letter is delightful in its quite unemotional commonplace, in its perfectly unvarnished homeliness, without a vestige of the vainglorious bravado of a stage-hero; and it gives us as clear an insight into the every-day life of this celebrated man as if we had peeped through one of the windows of his house, where the "herbe of grace" served as protector against the plague. But as to his art we are no wiser than we were before. Or does this entirely matter-of-fact letter confirm our supposition that Alleyn was a mere workman in art, who worked on a large scale? For this is how a strolling player or juggler might write to his family while travelling professionally from town to town. He does his work to

the best of his ability, and makes money by it, but his
thoughts are with his house and garden and with his
wife at home.

If chance some day should bring the unexpected to
pass and reveal a similar intimate epistle from Shakespeare, let us hope that the high-strung expectations
about his personality, in which our minds have been
reared, may not be disappointed by finding that he too
writes only about stockings and parsley.

Some lines of an answer from his father-in-law,
Henslowe, and from "the Mouse" will complete this
little still-life picture of the domestic existence of the
famous performer of villains during the terrible reign
of the plague.   The letters from home are written by a
"scrivener," as Mrs Alleyn probably could not write at
all, and Henslowe, as we know, wrote very badly.

> "For my wealbeloved husbande Mr. Edwarde
>   Allen, on of my Lorde Strange's players, this
>   be delyvered with speade.

> "Jesus.

"Welbeloved Sonne, Edwarde Allen, I and your
mother and your sister Beasse have all in generall our
hartie commendations unto you, and very glad to heare
of your good healthe, which we praye God to contenew
longe to his will and pleasur ; for we hard that you were
very sycke at Bathe, and that one of your felowes weare
fayn to playe your part for you, which wasse no lytell
greafe unto us to heare, but thanckes be to God for
amendmente, for we feared it much, because we had no
leatter from you when the other wifes had letters sente ;

which made your mouse not to weape a lytell, but tooke yt very greavesly, thinckinge that you had conseved some unkindnes of her, because you were ever wont to write with the firste : . . . Now, sonne [it is Henslowe who goes on] . . . and you sayd in your leater that she seant you not worde howe your garden and all your things dothe prosper; very well, thanckes be to God, for your beanes are growen to heg headge and well coded, and all other thinges doth very well . . . and for your good cownsell which you gave us in your leater we all thanck you, which wasse for keping of our howsse cleane and watringe of our dores, and strainge our windowes with wormwoode and rewe, which I hope all this we do and more ; for we strowe it with hartie prayers unto the lorde, which unto us is more avaylable than all thinges eallse in the world ; . . . and I praye ye, sonne, comend me harteley to all the reast of your fealowes in generall, for I growe poore for lacke of them, therefor have no geaftes to sende, but as good and faythfull a hart as they shall desyer to have comen amongst them. Now, sonne, we thanck you all for your tokens you seant us; and as for newes of the sycknes, I cane not seande you no juste note of yt, because ther is comandement to the contrary, but as I thincke doth die within the sittege and without of all syckneses to the number of seventeen or eyghten hundredth in one weacke . . .

    " Your lovinge Father and Mother to our powers,

        " P. H.   A.

  " Your lovinge wife to comande till death,

       " Johne Allen."

In the course of the autumn the plague ceased, and
about All Saints' Day (1st of November) Alleyn returned
from his tour with Lord Strange's company, which he
left for good in order to undertake the management of
"The Lord Admiral's Servants," afterwards "The
Prince's Men," to which he henceforth belonged. In
partnership with his father-in-law, the confirmed usurer
Henslowe, he now started a grand theatrical business in
"The Rose" Theatre and "The Bear-garden," an enterprise of which we have spoken in a previous chapter.
In 1597, when only thirty-one years of age, he had
already made sufficient money to allow him to retire
from the stage as an active player, which, however, he
only did for a time. When the sharp competition with
"The Globe" Theatre began, Alleyn returned to the
stage and acted again for some years—how many is
unknown—at the new "Fortune" theatre, which he and
his father-in-law had built.

Shortly after the accession of James I. the two
partners received a royal appointment as joint masters
of the Royal game of bears, bulls and mastiff dogs, an
office which Alleyn, who lived the longer of the two,
retained till his death, and which brought him in a considerable income. His riches increased from day to day;
he bought a mansion and grounds, and became the
recognised and unrivalled leader of the theatrical world.
This is shown by the innumerable petitions, humble
requests for loans, orders, etc., which abound among the
papers left by him. His fortune increased to such a
degree that he was able to buy the estate of Dulwich,
for which he paid in all £10,000. He became an

Esquire, and associated in the most familiar way with the highest aristocracy; the Earl of Arundel, for instance, and Sir William Alexander, were among his good friends.

But what gained him universal respect was the great munificence he exhibited in converting the Dulwich estate into a school and training college for poor children, an institution which still exists under its old name of "God's gift," and which continues to be one of the most largely attended schools in England.

An old legend tells us that in one of his parts—probably Dr Faustus—Alleyn had seen the devil in person appear before him on the stage, and that this had made him vow to spend his money on a charitable purpose. This, of course, is nonsense; but Alleyn, though twice married, was childless, and the great work of charity may have been a matter of honour as well as of feeling with him. He planned and arranged his college himself with the greatest care and with extraordinary practical sense. The study of his life and papers gives us the convincing impression that he was a distinguished man, and a firm and honest character. The letters of his later years especially testify to this fact. A short passage in one of them, where he maintains the honour of his class—not of his art—is aglow with pure manliness, and deserves to be known everywhere. The man of whom he had bought the Dulwich estate was a nobleman loaded with debts, Sir Francis Calton, who had wasted his patrimony. This Sir Francis gave him considerable annoyance, and, in his impotent vexation, had evidently—his letter is lost—

taunted Alleyn with his mean extraction and his pro-fession as an actor.   To this Alleyn replies :—

"And where you tell me of my poor originall and of my quality as a Player.   What is that ?   If I am richer than my auncesters, I hope I may be able to do more good with my riches than ever your auncesters did with their riches.   You must now beare povertye, and if you bear it more patiently than I, your desert will be the gretter.   That I was a player I can not deny, and I am sure I will not.   My meanes of living were honest, and with the poore abilytyes wherewith god blesst me I was able to doe something for myselfe, my relatives and my frendes, many of them nowe lyving at this daye will not refuse to owne what they owght me.   Therefore I am not ashamed."

After retiring from the theatre as an actor Alleyn lived a quiet domestic life, regularly gathered his dues from the theatres, cultivated his distinguished acquaint-ances, and entertained his former companions at little parties on his estate.   His most familiar friends among the actors seem to have been Benfield, Cartwright, Lowin, Taylor, and others, members also, as we see, of " The King's Company," though, of course, the "Fortune" company, "The Prince's Men," were more frequently invited.   He does not seem to have associated at all with contemporary authors, not even with those who had written for him, like Ben Jonson, Dekker, Middle-ton, Heywood, Webster or Marston.

Several of these, however, did not fail to express to him their great admiration of his dramatic art.   Jonson, for instance, dedicates an epigram[1] to him, in which,

[1] Ben Jonson : Epigrams, No. 89, ed. Gifford.

after the obligatory comparison with Roscius and Æsop, which is used for nearly all contemporary actors of note, appear the following lines :—

> " How can so great example die in me [viz., that of
>   Cicero, which brought the name of Roscius down
>   to posterity]
> That, Allen, I should pause to publish thee
> Who both their graces [that of Roscius and of Æsop]
>   in thyself hast more.
> Outstript, than they did all that went before,
> And present worth in all dost so contract,
> As others speak, but only thou dost act.
> Wear this renown.   'Tis just, that who did give
> To many poets life, by one should live."

It might be concluded from these verses that Alleyn also played comic parts, for Jonson knew quite well that Roscius was a comic actor.   Nor is it at all improbable that this was the case, for in those times it was not usual for actors to be limited to particular lines.   But we are unable to mention a single one of these parts.   An expression like "as others speak, but only thou dost act," must strike the eye.   Do they not confirm our supposition about Alleyn's excessive "action," which we cannot be surprised to hear was particularly to the taste of the rather coarse-grained Jonson?

Thomas Heywood, who during many years wrote for Alleyn's company, also speaks of him in the most enthusiastic terms.   First of all in his "Apology for Actors" (1612), where he says: "Among so many dead, let me not forget one yet alive, in his time the most worthy, famous Maister Edward Allen." [1]

And in the prologue of Marlowe's *Jew of Malta*, which he published in 1633, six years after the death of Alleyn,[2] he writes :—

> " We know not how our play may pass this stage,
>   But by the best of poets in that age
>   The Malta Jew had being and was made ;
>   And he then by the best of actors play'd.
>   In Hero and Leander one did gain
>   A lasting memory : in Tamberlaine,
>   This Jew, with others many, the other man
>   The attribute of peerless ; being a man
>   Whom we may rank with (doing no one wrong)
>   Proteus for shapes, and Roscius for a tongue,
>   So could he speak, so vary."

Edward Alleyn died in 1625, on the 25th of November, at the age of sixty.   Two years before his death, and five months after losing his first wife, he married a young girl, Constance Donne, a daughter of the well-known clergyman, Dr John Donne.   With Dr Donne, however, he lived in constant enmity, and therefore left him nothing in his will ; while he generously bestowed £100 on the former proprietor of Dulwich, besides forgiving a debt of £20.   He is buried in his college, which

---

[1] Thomas Heywood : *An Apology for Actors*, p. 43.
[2] A short time before the play had been revived at " The Cockpit " with R. Perkins in the part of Barrabas.

13—Edward Alleyn (after a picture at Dulwich College).

is also the repository of a number of curiosities illus-
trating the history of the stage—among others, the portrait reproduced above.[1]

III

The Shakespearean School— Shakespeare as Actor—Richard Burbage and
his Company—Nathaniel Field—The Cessation of Plays.

Nowadays Shakespeare's relation to the art of acting
is generally considered to have been of a purely business-
like and very cool nature, as a tie which he longed to
break, and which he really broke as soon as he was
capable of doing so. But this view of the matter rests
on a great and evident mistake.

It is quite natural that Shakespeare's eminent poetic
productions should have entirely eclipsed the remembrance

---

[1] All the material we possess concerning the life of Alleyn is chiefly
found in Collier's *Memoirs of Edward Alleyn*, London, 1841. But this
book, like so many by the same author, is marred by a number of spurious
documents, which are mixed up with much good and genuine matter. As a
guide to the unprepared reader, I will mention some of the grossest forgeries: p. 13, the poem "Sweete Ned," etc., is altogether spurious; p. 45,
in the letter from Henslowe some words are introduced about Thomas
Lodge to prove that he was an actor (and hauinge some knowledge and
acquaintance of him as a player); p. 63, to the otherwise genuine letter
from Alleyn's wife a forged note has been added about Shakespeare (Mr
Shakespeare of the globe, who came . . .); p. 69, the list of the eleven
actors of "The King's Company" is concocted by Collier (a facsimile of
the forged document is found in Lee's *Life of Shakespeare*, libr. ed., p. 305);
pp. 90 ff., the list of poor-rates, which is meant to prove that Shakespeare
lived in Southwark in 1609, is fallacious. The whole work is brimful of
false information about stage-matters. Fleay somewhere mentions having
found more than one hundred misstatements merely in the account of
Kemp. The number would be at least equally great if he took Alleyn's
Memoirs alone.

of his histrionic art.   It must not be forgotten, however, that as certainly as he figures in the modern eye as the great poet who also at times played comedy, so certainly did he appear to his own time as the excellent actor and stage-manager, who also wrote plays, much more so than even Ben Jonson, who was also an actor.

Clearly enough, his poetic fame gradually eclipsed his reputation as an actor.   In 1592, when Shakespeare was a young man of twenty-four, Chettle writes about him that he is " exelent in the qualitie he professes." [1] His somewhat younger colleague, William Beeston, the manager of a company which for a time was called " The Beeston Boys," afterwards told Aubrey that he acted exceedingly well.   But already in 1699 we learn from the anonymous author of *Historia Histrionica* that he was a much better author than actor.   And Nicholas Rowe, the Shakespeare publisher, tells us in 1709 that he distinguished himself, if not as a superior actor, yet as an excellent author.

In the nineteenth century Guizot,[2] among others, writes (1852): " As an actor he does not seem to have distinguished himself among his rivals."   Till now it has been assumed that his profession as actor weighed on him like a nightmare of shame, which he fervently longed to throw off.

This opinion is based on a few passages in the *Sonnets*, which poems, on the whole, have given rise to all kinds of fancies, some of which are perfectly absurd,

---

[1] The word " quality" in the language of the time is constantly used in the sense of acting.   Compare, *e.g.*, *Hamlet*, ii. 2 : " come, give us a taste of your quality."   [2] *Shakespeare et son temps*, p. 61.

about the life and circumstances of Shakespeare.[1]   Thus
No. XXIX., which begins with these lines :—

> " When in disgrace with fortune and men's eyes,
>   I all alone beweep my outcast state,
>   And trouble deaf heaven with my bootless cries,
>   And look upon myself and curse my fate. . . . "

and CX., where he says :—

> " Alas, 'tis true, I have gone here and there,
>   And made myself a motley to the view."

or again, the bitter lines in CXI. :—

> " O for my sake do you with Fortune chide,
>   The guilty goddess of my harmful deeds.
>   That did not better for my life provide,
>   Than public means, which public manners breeds.
>   Thence comes it that my name receives a brand,
>   And almost thence my nature is subdued
>   To what it works in, like the dyer's hand. . . . "

But these testimonies do not go far to prove that
Shakespeare had no love for histrionic art.   If, on the
whole, it can be considered as anything more than a
momentary feeling, which was consciously clothed in a
poetic form, what he complains of, with less firm
manliness than Alleyn, but certainly with stronger
emotion, was no more than his social status and the
disgust which every actor, and especially the gifted one,
may occasionally feel with his relation to the public.

We cannot wonder that Shakespeare, who was

---

[1] Mr Israel Gollancz, the editor of *The Temple Shakespeare*, very wittily
puts at the heads of the Sonnets five different and quite contradictory
mottoes (by Wordsworth, Browning, Swinburne, Shelley and Tennyson).

evidently ambitious and aspiring, not merely in his art, but also from a mere worldly and social point of view, found his class low, compared with the powerful and glorious position of an Earl of Southampton or of Pembroke—to whichever of these two the Sonnets may have been addressed.

As a matter of fact he retired early from the theatre, at the age of about forty-six; but so did many of his colleagues, who, when they had made a certain amount of money, withdrew to rest after the hard toil of a number of years. For at that time, even more than nowadays, the actor's work was most fatiguing; and this, we suppose, may be the reason why many of the actors of those days died comparatively young.[1] The companies were small, and the répertoire exceedingly large. So there was much to be learned, and it had to be learned well, as the actors had not, as nowadays, a prompter to support them. In addition to this, Shakespeare had his great work as an author, and undoubtedly was stage-manager—at least with regard to his own plays. Life as well as work moved at full speed in those times; no wonder that age and fatigue came early. But Shakespeare continued his work as an actor faithfully and uninterruptedly until he retired altogether from the theatrical world, giving up authorship as well as acting. That he loved his art and was more interested

---

[1] Shakespeare and Richard Burbage were fifty-two years old when they died; Nathaniel Field forty-six, Robert Arnim about forty-three. John Underwood can scarcely have been forty, and William Ostler not much more than thirty. Kemp and Tarlton no doubt also died young, whereas Edward Alleyn, who, it is true, spent a large part of his life away from the theatre, lived to the age of sixty.

14—William Shakespeare (from the Bust belonging to the Garrick Club).

in it than most of his fellow-actors we shall shortly try
to prove.

Shakespeare's theatrical career, in its external
features, is very clear and simple. Only the first years
after his arrival in London are obscure, or rather,
absolutely blank. There is no foundation whatever for
all the legends about his beginning his stage life by
holding the horses of the spectators during the performance, by organising a company of boys for this
purpose, by helping the book-holder as call-boy, who
had to summon the actors when they were to appear on
the stage. All these reports are of very late origin, and
the thought that they might possibly be true is certainly
no sufficient reason for accepting them as such.

But from the moment when he enters into the full
light of stage history till he retires to his native town,
tired of the labour and toil of London life, his career is
as plain as possible. During all these twenty years he
belongs uninterruptedly to the same company, which, at
the beginning of his career was " Lord Strange's," and
at the end of it " The King's Men."

At the age of twenty-eight we see him already—it
must be borne in mind that he began comparatively late
—in an undoubtedly distinguished position as actor and
author, with steadily increasing fame, and, as is always
the case, surrounded by a barking host of enviers.

One of these, Robert Greene, an author of some
talent, was now a miserable invalid, ruined by a vicious
life, the end of which was near. According to his own
saying, he was now converted, and with the usual
inclination of proselytes to attack their former friends,

he made haste before his death to compose a libellous
pamphlet against his old colleagues among authors and
actors.   He warns his friends Marlowe, Lodge (or
Nash) and Peele against the sinful writing of plays, but
especially against actors.

" Base-minded men," he says, "all three of you, if by
my miserie ye be not warned ; for unto none of you, like
me, sought those burres to cleave ; those puppits, I
meane, that speak from our mouths, those anticks gar-
nisht in our colours.   Is it not strange that I, to whom
they all have beene beholding, shall, were ye in that case
that I am now, be both at once of them forsaken ?   Yes,
trust them not ; for there is an upstart crow, beautified
with our feathers, that with his Tyger's heart wrapt in a
Player's hide, supposes he is as well able to bumbast out
of blanke verse as the best of you ; and being an absolute
Johannes Factotum, is in his owne conseite the onely
Shake-scene in a countrie.   O that I might intreate
your rare wits to be imployed in more profitable courses,
and let these apes imitate your past excellence, and
never more acquaint them with your admired inventions !

.   .   .   .

.   .   .   .

.   .   .   Wilst you may, seeke you better
maisters ; for it is pittie men of such rare wits should
be subject to the pleasures of such rude groomes. . . .
For other newcommers I leave them to the mercie of
these painted monsters." [1]

---

[1] Greene's *Groat's worth of Wit, bought with a Million of Repentaunce.*
The book appeared in September 1592, very shortly after Greene's death ; the
passage quoted is taken from the introductory letter.

What made Greene direct this fanatical attack against "Lord Strange's Men"—for there can be no doubt that it was aimed at this company—we are unable to say. Surely it was more than mere professional jealousy. Most likely he had had a theatrical conflict with "Lord Strange's Men," who, during the first half of 1592, acted at "The Rose" Theatre, and had performed plays by Marlowe, Lodge and Peele, while their greatest success had been the first part of *Henry VI.*, in which Shakespeare's Talbot-scenes had called forth special enthusiasm from the public.

The literary basis of Greene's attack does not concern us here. We have quoted it much more at length than in the ordinary literary handbooks, in order to show that it is Shakespeare the actor whom he wants to hit; he does not consider Shakespeare as an author at all. What strikes him is, that having appeared but recently, he has gained ascendency in his company, and has become an absolute factotum; so much so, that he has even ventured to drive an older noted author and actor into a corner.

A few months later this personal attack on Shakespeare received a warm retort from Henry Chettle, who says in the preface of his "Kind Harts Dreame": "About three moneths since died Mr Robert Greene, leaving many papers in sundry booke-sellers hands, among other his Groatsworth of Wit, in which a letter written to divers play-makers, is offensively by one or two of them taken; and because on the dead they cannot be avenged, they wilfully forge in their conceites a living author; and after tossing it two and fro, no remedy but it must light on me.   How I have all the time of my conversing in printing hindred the bitter inveying against schollers, it hath been very well knowne; and how in that I dealt, I can sufficiently proove.   With neither of them that take offence was I acquainted, and with one of them I care not if I never be.   The other, whome at that time I did not so much spare as since I wish I had, for that, as I have moderated the heate of living writers, and might have usde my owne discretion,—especially in such a case, the author beeing dead,—that I did not I am sory as if the originall fault had beene my fault, because myselfe have seene his demeanor no less civill, than he exelent in the qualitie he professes;—besides, divers of worship have reported his uprightnes of dealing, which argues his honesty and his facetious grace in writing, that aprooves his art."

The attack and the defence combined give us a clear idea of the young actor Shakespeare as a man of great importance to his company, a man of the future on whom high expectations were built.   Except the short period of occasional engagements at "The Rose," and afterwards (in 1594) at "The Newington," and several journeys in the provinces, Shakespeare during his first period chiefly played at "The Theatre."

When "The Globe" was built in 1599, the proprietors, the brothers Burbage, as we said above, admitted Shakespeare and some of his distinguished colleagues as part-owners of the theatre.   After 1608 he acted also at "Blackfriars," which at this time was used by "The King's Men," till three years later he definitely retired to Stratford a wealthy man.

Unfortunately we know next to nothing about the parts he acted. That he played tragedy as well as comedy we see from the list of actors of two of Ben Jonson's plays. Among the *dramatis personae* of *Every Man in His Humour* we read of "the principal Comedians" who have acted in this excellent play. Will Shakespeare stands at the top. Is this done in courtesy to Shakespeare, because it was he who caused the play to be acted? is it mere chance? or does it mean that Shakespeare acted the part which headed the list of the persons represented?

The last suggestion seems to be the most probable, and in this case we find that Shakespeare performed Old Knowell, a rather important part in the play, a "heavy father," which afterwards belonged in Germany to the popular Biedermann-répertoire of Iffland and Schröder.

In *Sejanus* we see Shakespeare fifth among the principal Tragedians, at the top of the second column of the eight actors, and opposite to him Richard Burbage, who heads the first column. So, if the conclusion we drew above is right, he must have acted a rather inferior part in this play.

Rowe tells us that Shakespeare represented the dead king's ghost in *Hamlet*, and that it was the top of his performance, to which may be added the statement of John Davies, that he performed " some kingly parts." [1]

---

[1] " Some say, good Will, which I in sport do sing,
  Hadst thou not play'd some kingly parts in sport,
  Thou hadst been a companion for a king."
          The Scourge of Folly, by John Davies of Hereford ;
          quoted by Malone : *Historical Account*, p. 237.

brother of Shakespeare's, who was old and infirm at the time, but who could still remember that, when young, he had seen William act the octogenarian servant Adam in *As You Like It.*

This is absolutely all that is known about the parts which Shakespeare performed, and it is perfectly useless to try to guess what parts he may have taken. Even though we know beforehand that in most of his own plays he did not represent the principal characters, there is a large field for conjecture. To judge from the parts already mentioned, we might conclude that he had especially impersonated old men, but the fact that two parts are known, and two others are supposed to have been old men, is not sufficient foundation for this conclusion, seeing that during his twenty years' career as an actor he must have played at least some hundred parts.

But of his relation to the art of acting in general, we know, or may learn something more from his plays. It is a foregone conclusion that dramatic art filled his life, as he was attached to it in a threefold way, as poet, as actor, and as stage-manager. That it filled his thoughts also we see from innumerable images scattered throughout his works, which are derived from dramatic art and stage-life. To him "All the world's a stage— And all the men and women merely players; They have their exits and their entrances; And one man in his time plays many parts, His acts being seven ages."[1]

How fully he realised and yet wondered at the overwhelming power which the art of the genuine actor could Finally, we have a statement of Gilbert, a younger

[1] *As You Like It,* ii. 7.

exercise on himself and others, we find most strikingly expressed in the following speech of Hamlet :—

" Is it not monstrous that this player here,
But in a fiction, in a dream of passion,
Could force his soul so to his own conceit
That from her working all his visage warm'd,
Tears in his eyes, distraction in's aspect,
A broken voice, and his whole function suiting
With forms to his conceit? and all for nothing !
    For Hecuba !
What's Hecuba to him, or he to Hecuba,
That he should weep for her." [1]

But in his relations to the art of acting Shakespeare is not only the philosophic critic, but also the practical reformer. We have seen him, when quite young, deriding the unreal, empty and bombastic style, for which in his maturer years his contempt increases and deepens. His taste develops in refinement, and he maintains his ambition against the cheap applause of the mob, which is too frequently bought with false coin ; he does not appreciate the laughter which the comic actor earns with his shallow jokes, if they are not in keeping with the subject of the play and disturb its sense ; nor is he impressed by a hero who leaves the stage in a boisterous, ostentatious way followed by the applauding cheers of the crowd, while he himself and every quiet expert shake their heads at the man's atrocious style of speaking. Just as it was his vocation as a poet to introduce artistic refinement, natural grace, deep feeling and genuine

[1] *Hamlet*, ii. 1.

humour into the old rude and ungraceful plays, so it became his task as an actor to lead the violent and affected style of acting back to nature, true feeling and moderation.   He did not wish to introduce a conventional literary taste, like that in which Goethe indulged when he wanted to reform the German acting, nor did he desire a sombre and dull indifference to counterbalance excessive enthusiasm and exaggerated praise ; all he wanted was naturalness.

Hamlet : " Be not too tame neither, but let your own discretion be your tutor : suit the action to the word, the word to the action ; with this special observance, that you o'erstep not the modesty of nature ; for anything so overdone is from the purpose of playing, whose end both at the first and now, was and is, to hold, as 'twere, the mirror up to nature; to show virtue her own feature, scorn her own image, and the very age and body of the time his form and pressure.   Now this overdone, or come tardy off, though it make the unskilful laugh, cannot but make the judicious grieve, the censure of the which one must in your allowance o'erweigh a whole theatre of others." [1]

It is Shakespeare who speaks these words, because they are burning on his tongue ; not Hamlet, for Hamlet at the moment has other things weighing more heavily on his mind than the duty of giving golden rules for their art to the actors he admires.

And the imperious and authoritative tone in which he speaks the words, and those we quoted above, is not that of a prince addressing poor actors, still less, of

[1] Act ii. Sc. 3.

course, that of an amateur to an old expert in his art. It is the language of the mature, intelligent, consistent actor to younger or less intelligent fellow-actors, or that of a teacher to his pupils. It is Shakespeare, the instructor, teaching his colleagues.

Perhaps this is an ideal picture; perhaps it was thus Shakespeare would have liked to speak to the other actors without having an opportunity of doing so. Perhaps the picture represents a fact; perhaps he did catch the ear of his fellow-actors, and was allowed to be their guide along the lofty but bewildering paths of art, which he knew better than anyone else; along which he himself preferred to walk, rather than on the broad and dusty road that leads to the favour of the pit.

We have, indeed, an absolute proof of the fact that Shakespeare did instruct his younger colleagues. Downes[1] tells us that when Thomas Betterton, the famous tragedian of the Restoration, was to play Hamlet, he was taught all the details by Sir William Davenant (Shakespeare's godson), who had seen the part performed by Mr Taylor of the Blackfriars' company, "he having been instructed by the author, Mr William Shakespeare"; and by his exact reproduction Betterton gained a higher respect and reputation than any other.

If Shakespeare instructed young Joseph Taylor, when he was to play Hamlet, he no doubt also gave his assistance to his contemporary, his friend and comrade, Richard Burbage, who was the original performer of the part. On the whole, we may conclude that these

[1] The author of *Roscius Anglicanus.*

two men, the highly gifted poet and the equally intelligent actor, worked together in hearty co-operation; they inspired and incited each other to continuous new efforts, and the result obtained must have been wonderful.

It has frequently been imagined that the histrionic art of those days was something barbarous and childlike, something which our taste is much too advanced to appreciate. Unfortunately we have not the slightest chance of settling this question by evidence. But since none of the other arts, poetry, painting, sculpture, applied arts—perhaps with the single exception of music—stand higher now than they did at the time of the Renaissance, it would be absurd to imagine that the art of acting, which is not one of those which require centuries of cultivation before they can attain perfection, should not have failed to reach an equally high standard with poetry, especially since England offered the very best conditions for its thriving.

In Italy and France, poetry and the art of acting were still too far apart to obtain a great result. The actors cultivated "pure dramatic art" with improvisations and set phrases, and they reached a certain external perfection, while the poets who enjoyed any consideration wrote learned pseudo-classical dramas, which nobody beyond their own circle wanted to see performed; and they had, in consequence, a great contempt for the theatre.

In England, on the contrary, poetry and dramatic art went to work hand in hand; indeed, they were so merged into each other that we are frequently at a loss to know whether it is the poet who acts or the actor who composes.   Men like Marlowe, Robert Wilson, Greene, Shakespeare, Jonson, Field, and many others—men, that is, whose aim in life it was to create art on the stage both by writing and by acting, these were the men who raised dramatic art in England.

But no doubt it is permissible to say that the co-operation between Shakespeare and Burbage, and the effect it exercised on the company to which they belonged, was the culmination of the whole movement. In the eyes of the time, therefore, at any rate from the close of the nineties, Burbage's company was unquestionably the best and the finest in London.

Richard Burbage was a child of the stage, a son of the old actor James, the first builder of theatres in England.   Of course he was brought up as an actor from his childhood, while Cuthbert,[1] the elder brother, who seems to have been an intelligent and business-like man, became a bookseller.   And, very likely, the old joiner and artist initiated him in the mysteries of the "art," as he understood them, and as they were expounded in his days.   We find Richard, when very young, already appearing in *The Seven Deadly Sins*,[2] the improvisational and spectacular play by Tarlton, and it is not unlikely that during his earliest years James Burbage's répertoire consisted largely of that kind of play.   But with the increasing influence of Shakespeare, the répertoire no doubt underwent a change for the

---

[1] "Cuthbert Burby" he generally calls himself in the books he publishes.
[2] His name is sometimes met with in the scenario, but it is impossible to find out which part he played.

III.

better. Shakespeare was three or four years older than Richard Burbage ;[1] this circumstance, combined with the great superiority of his mind, rendered it natural that he should obtain enough influence over the young actor to draw him away from the affected and boisterous manner which was the fashion of the time, and inoculate him with the sound principles which ruled his own writing and acting. Very likely Shakespeare did not feel himself qualified for the great principal parts of his own plays ; it seems evident from what we know of him, that his nature was too delicate and gentle for such violent characters as Richard III., Shylock, Othello and Macbeth. At any rate, it is certain that it became Richard Burbage's task to play all these parts, and that he played them so excellently that he gained the highest admiration from all his contemporaries. But it was not only these striking and violent characters in which he was so successful ; he played Prince Henry, Hamlet and Brutus with equal success. In 1664 Flecknoe[2] says : "He was a delightful Proteus, so wholly transforming himself into his parts, and putting off himself with his cloaths, as he never (not so much as in the tyring-house) assumed himself again, untill the play was done. He had all the parts of an excellent orator, animating his words with speaking, and speech with action ; his auditors being never more delighted than when he spake, nor more sorry than when he held his peace ; yet even then he was an excellent actor still :

[1] The exact date of Richard Burbage's birth is unknown, but he must have been born about 1567.

[2] Flecknoe : *A Short Discourse of the English Stage*, 1664 ; *cf.* Malone : *Historical Account*, p. 240.

never failing in his part when he had done speaking, but with his looks and gesture maintaining it still to the height."

These are general terms, but they give an idea of the style of Burbage's art. We see that he did not belong to the class of actors who transform the part to suit their own person, but on the contrary to those who adapt their persons to their parts;[1] and that he eagerly and conscientiously gave himself up to his art.

A funeral elegy, written after the death of Richard Burbage in 1619, is preserved in several manuscripts and reprinted in various places. J. P. Collier pretends to have found a copy of this elegy, which enumerates a large number of the parts acted by Burbage; out of Shakespeare alone, for instance, it gives Shylock, Richard III., Prince Henry, Romeo, Henry V., Brutus, Hamlet, Othello, Lear, Macbeth, Pericles and Coriolanus; whereas the other copies do not mention these parts. Now, though this addition to the elegy, as far as I know, has not been proved to be a forgery,[2] and though it has been introduced as an authentic fact by nearly all writers on these questions, the mere form of this list of parts bears in my eyes such a distinct stamp of being spurious, that, considering the notorious untrustworthiness of the writer, it is wiser for the present not to put faith in this testimony of the famous actor's parts.

Burbage very likely acted these and several other

[1] In modern times the former category seems to be the prevalent one, at all events with the great celebrities (among them, for instance, Eleonora Duse, Mounet-Sully, Josef Kainz).

[2] The whole elegy is reprinted in Collier's *English Dramatic Poetry*, iii. 299-302.

parts, but we only know with absolute certainty that he played Hamlet, Hieronymo (in Kyd), King Lear, Othello, which are mentioned in the authentic manuscripts of the elegy, and Richard III. An undoubtedly genuine version of the elegy contains these lines :—[1]

" Hee's gone, and with him what a world is dead,
   Which hee reviv'd ; to bee revived so
   No more :—young Hamlet, old Hieronimo,
   Kind Leir, the greived Moor, and more beside
   That lived in him, have now for ever died.
   Oft have I seene him leape into the grave,
   Suiting the person (that he seemed to have)
   Of a sad lover with so true an eye,
   That then I would have sworn hee meant to die."

As to Richard III. we know from several contemporary anecdotes that this part was performed by Burbage. One of these, told by the lawyer, John Manningham, in his diary on March 1602, is well known ; it runs as follows : " Upon a time when Burbidge played Rich. 3., there was a citizen grene soe farr in liking with him that, before shee went from the play, shee appointed him to come that night unto her by the name of Ri. the 3. Shakespere, overhearing their conclusion, went before, was entertained, and at his game ere Burbedge came. Then message being brought that Rich. the 3d. was at the dore, Shakespeare caused returne to be made that William the Conquerorer was before Rich. the 3. Shakespere's name William."[1]

---

[1] Reprinted in Halliwell-Phillipps : *Outlines*, pp. 600 f.

Another anecdote which shows the popularity of
Burbage in this part, and which is generally misquoted,
is told in a versified book of travels by Bishop Corbet.[1]
On his journey the bishop arrives at Bosworth Plain,
where once the battle was fought between Richard III.
and Richmond.   The keeper of the inn where the bishop
is staying is a loquacious man, " full of ale and history."
He can describe the whole battle.   In short, he can tell
within an inch where Richmond stood and where Richard
fell.   But the prelate soon finds out that the landlord has
derived his knowledge from seeing the play :—

" But chiefly by that one perspicuous thing
   Where he mistook a player for a king,
   For when he would have said, King Richard dy'd,
   And call'd a horse, a horse, he Burbage cry'd."

Though we cannot tell for certain what parts Burbage
performed, we read his name in the lists of characters
of several contemporary dramatic authors, *e.g.*, in Jonson's
Sejanus, in which we imagine that he acted the principal
part, and in *Every Man in His Humour*, in which he
probably played the jealous husband, Kitely.   In Marston's *Malcontent* we know for a fact he represented
Malevole, the exiled Duke of Genoa, at the time when
this play passed from the hands of the " Children of the
Chapel " at " The Blackfriars " to " The King's Men " at
" The Globe."   In the Induction which Webster wrote
for the occasion, and which we have quoted in a previous
chapter (compare above, p. 121), Burbage appears in

---

[1] Published in 1647, but written much earlier.   The passage which contains this anecdote is reprinted in Halliwell-Phillipps : *Outlines*, pp. 601 ff.

person under his own name, and offers his welcome to the gallants on the stage.   When he retires one of the dandies (Sinklo) says : " Does he play the Malcontent? " to which Condell, who also appears under his own name, replies : " Yes, sir." [1]

The external facts of Richard Burbage's theatrical career were as simple as Shakespeare's, or even simpler. He was attached to the same company throughout, first as actor, and later, after the death of his father, as manager and proprietor as well.   His relations with the various theatres have been mentioned above in detail. Of his private life and character, we know nothing beyond that he was married and had several children, and that he became a man of considerable means. We have spoken of his financial condition on a previous occasion.

Like many actors after him, he cultivated pictorial as well as dramatic art, and the portrait reproduced here, the original of which is in the Dulwich Museum, is supposed to have been painted by himself.   It shows a pair of dark, melancholy eyes ; a thin, sensitive mouth ; and a large, fleshy nose.   He is said to have been some-what short of stature, and rather stout.   It is supposed, as we know, that the phrase used about Hamlet, " He's fat and scant o' breath," spoken by the Queen during the duel, alludes to Burbage.   The fact that he died of apoplexy comparatively young (at the age of fifty-two) also seems to bear witness to his increasing stoutness. First of all his tongue was paralysed, and thence the

---

[1] John Marston : *The Malcontent*, Induction, Bullen's edition, i. 204.

paralysis gradually extended to his whole body, as we learn from the dirge on his death :—[1]

"Hadst thou but spoke to Death, and us'd the power
Of thy enchanting tongue, at that first hour
Of his assault, he had let fall his dart,
And quite been charm'd with thy all-charming art ;
This Death well knew, and, to prevent this wrong,
He first made seizure on thy wondrous tongue,
Then on the rest, 'twas easy ; by degrees
The slender ivy twines the hugest trees."

His death, which occurred on May 13th, 1619, called forth such universal grief in London that it seemed to make people forget the death of the Queen,[2] which had occurred a few weeks previously. A little poem, no doubt hailing from the Puritan side, but very well written indeed, derides the difference of feeling shown by the Londoners on the two mournful events, and declares it scandalous that

"The deaths of men who act our Queens and Kings
Are now more mourn'd than are the real things.
The Queen is dead ! to him now what are Queens,
Queens of the theatre are much more worth,
Drawn to the play-house by the bawdy scenes
To revel in the foulness they call mirth.
Dick Burbage was their mortal god on earth ;
When he expires, lo ! all lament the man,
But where's the grief should follow good Queen Anne."[3]

[1] The title of this elegy is : *On Mr Richard Burbidg, an excellent both player and painter.*

[2] Queen Anne, wife of James I., died on the first of March 1619.

[3] J. P. Collier : *English Dramatic Poetry*, iii. 303.

Round Shakespeare and Burbage were gathered a number of actors of whose individual artistic characters we know nothing or next to nothing, but whose names have been frequently mentioned in these pages : men of the old school, like Augustine Phillips, Thomas Pope, and George Bryan; Shakespeare's intimate friends of about his own age, Henry Condell and John Heminge, two highly trusted members of the Company; Heminge being, according to tradition, the original performer of Falstaff, Condell perhaps the first Captain Bobadill in Jonson's *Every Man in his Humour*.   Both of them can lay claim to the deepest gratitude of posterity for their edition of their friend Shakespeare's plays, without which, certainly, some of them would never have reached us.   Besides these we find a younger generation, including men like Joseph Taylor and Nathaniel Field, Burbage's successors in the tragic line; John Lowin, Heminge's successor in the old comic characters, the original Volpone in Jonson's comedy of that name; the clown Robert Arnim, of Tarlton's school, who filled the blank left by William Kemp; William Sly, whom we know best from the amusing Induction of Marston's *Malcontent*, in which he played the comic gallant, who forcibly obtains admission to the stage; and John Shancke, who in the thirties occupied a distinguished position, and was the most important shareholder in both "The Blackfriars" and "The Globe"; finally the performers of female parts : Robert Goughe or Goffe, Alexander Cooke, who played both tragic and comic female characters, and was a pupil of Heminge; and the charming Richard Robinson, who, like Shancke, in

15—Richard Burbage (after a picture at Dulwich College supposed to have been painted by himself).

1635, held a large number of shares in the two theatres
of the company.[1]

The latter is mentioned in a characteristic manner by
Ben Jonson in his *The Devil is an Ass*, in which the two
rascals, Meercraft and Engine, are discussing the best
means of procuring a woman to help them in deceiving
the foolish squire, Fitzdottrel. The conversation runs
as follows :—

Engine : " Why, sir, your best will be one o' the
                players."

Meercraft : " No, there is no trusting them. They'll
                talk on't
                And tell their poets."

Engine : " What if they do? the jest
                Will brook the stage. But there be some
                of 'em
                Are very honest lads. There is Dick
                Robinson,
                A very pretty fellow, and comes often
                To a gentleman's chamber, a friend of
                mine : we had
                The merriest supper of it there one night.
                The gentleman's landlady invited him
                To a gossip's feast : now, he, sir, brought
                Dick Robinson,
                Drest like a lawyer's wife, amongst 'em
                all.
                (I lent him clothes), but to see him
                behave it,

---

[1] Compare the repeatedly quoted complaint from the actors Benfield, etc.,
reprinted in Halliwell-Phillipps : *Outlines*, p. 542.

> And lay the law, and carve, and drink
> unto 'em,
> And then talk bawdy, and send frolics!
> O!
> It would have burst your buttons, or not
> left you
> A seame."

Meercraft. " They say he's an ingenious youth."

Engine. " O, sir ! and dresses himself the best, beyond
Forty o' your very ladies ! Did you never
see him ? "

Meercraft. " No, I do seldom see those toys." [1]

This is one of the very few pieces of contemporary evidence of what we should consider the unsavoury manner in which the actors of female parts behaved themselves off the stage.

Among the actors above-mentioned there was one who belonged to " The King's Men " for only a very short time, but who, nevertheless, acquired great fame, Nathaniel Field, whose name has appeared repeatedly in these pages.

Field was an actor of rather a remarkable type, who stands a little removed from the men whom we have chosen above as types of the histrionic art of the time. On this account he deserves a few lines to himself, though we must acknowledge that we know nothing distinctive about his style of acting.

The first remarkable circumstance relating to Field is his parentage. He was the son of a Puritan preacher,

---

[1] Ben Jonson : *The Devil is an Ass*, ii. 3. Gifford's edition.

one of the most ardent opponents of the art to which his son afterwards devoted his life, the same Rev. John Field, who, in 1583, saw a judgment of God in the misfortune that happened in Paris Garden, when the Bear-garden, which was situated there, collapsed on a Sunday.

Fortunately for him, he did not live to see his son follow the way of evil, as he died the year after the birth of Nathaniel (1587). At the age of ten the latter was apprenticed to a bookseller, but no doubt was very early pressed to enter as a chorister among the Queen's Chapel-boys.[1] And here, between the ages of twelve and fourteen, he already gained unusual celebrity. Ben Jonson, who, as we have seen, was writing for the Chapel-boys at "The Blackfriars" during these years, took charge of the clever and talented boy, taught him Latin,[2] and, no doubt, instructed him in acting. For Jonson was known as a bad actor, but as an excellent instructor. Field became the principal actor in *Cynthia's Revels* and in the *Poetaster*, in which Jonson puts his name first among the boys. At the dates of their production he was respectively thirteen and fourteen years old, and not only a noted actor, but in the heat of the literary quarrel, with Jonson to back him.

[1] At that time Queen Elizabeth had appointed a committee with the task of procuring boys for the school of choristers of the Chapel Royal. The Committee made a bargain with "The Blackfriars" Theatre and its leader, Henry Evans, for providing the latter with the necessary boy-actors. In this matter Evans overstepped the limits of his authority by depriving parents of the control of their children. This brought about a lawsuit between Evans and a Suffolk gentleman. The latter gained his cause, and Evans lost his privilege. The deeds concerning this affair have been published by Mr James Greenstreet in *The Athenæum* of August 10th, 1889. See above, pp. 45 f.

[2] *Jonson's Conversations with Drummond*, p. 11.

However, he did not share the ordinary fate of infant prodigies, and fade away on reaching maturity ; on the contrary, he continued to develop as an actor and as a poet. Before long he remains the only actor whose fame can be compared to that of Richard Burbage, for by this time Alleyn had retired from the stage, and he became the author of a number of very popular plays, which he wrote, partly alone, partly in co-operation with Fletcher, Massinger and Daborne. A well-known play of his is the amusing comedy *Woman is a Weathercock*, which was performed about 1610 by the company to which Field continued to belong, and which at that time was called " The Children of the Queen's Revels," who now acted in the refectory of Whitefriars, after " The King's Men " had taken possession of " The Blackfriars." In the preface of this play we find the rather haughty remark that he does not wish to dedicate it to any great personage, as he does not care for the 40s. which he might expect to receive as a gratuity.

A short time afterwards we find him in the clutches of old Henslowe, and by now he has changed his tune. As we stated before, in 1613 he was engaged by Henslowe and Alleyn as principal actor at the newly built " Hope " Theatre. Here he had a very good situation indeed, and Henslowe evidently treated him as a star to whom particular consideration was due ; [1] for all that he was soon in debt to the cunning manager, who had even to rescue him from the debtors' prison. A letter from Field concerning this affair has been

[1] This appears from the complaint previously quoted from the other actors against Henslowe.

preserved among the *Alleyn Papers*.[1] It runs as follows :—

" Father Hinchlow,

" I am unluckily taken on an execution of 30 l. I can be discharged for xx l. x l I have from a friend ; if now, in my extremity, you will venture x l more for my liberty, I will never share penny till you have it againe, and make any satisfaction by writing or otherwise, y[t] you can devise. I am loath to importune, because I know your disbursements are great ; nor must any know I send to you, for then my creditor will not free me but for the whole some. I pray, speedily consider my occasion, for if I be putt to use other meanes, I hope all men and selfe will excuse me if (unforcedly) I cannot proove so honest as towards you I ever resolv'd to be.

" Yo[r] loving son,[2]

" Nat. Field."

After the death of Henslowe in 1616, Field left " The Hope" Theatre and Alleyn's company and joined " The King's Men." With him went Fletcher, Massinger and Jonson as authors, which testifies to the favour in which he stood at that time. But he did not remain long with " The King's Men " either ; after 1619, at all events, we hear nothing about him as an actor. We should have thought that the death of Burbage, which

[1] *Alleyn Papers*, pp. 65 f.

[2] It was a custom in those times for the young to address their elders with whom they stood in friendly relations as "father," and *vice versâ* for older people to call the younger ones "sons." Henslowe is frequently called Father Henslowe by younger actors and authors, to whom he advanced money.

occurred this same year, would have opened new fields
to him in his own line.   But, most likely, Joseph Taylor
took possession of the parts for which Field considered
himself particularly qualified; we know that Taylor
played Hamlet after Burbage, and Field may have felt
offended and retired altogether.

We know of one Shakespearean part which he played,
that of Othello, from a malicious little epigram,[1] which
sneers at Field's jealousy of his wife.   We quote it
here :—

> " Field is, in sooth, an actor, all men know it,
>   And is the true Othello of the poet.
>   I wonder if 'tis true, as people tell us,
>   That like the character, he is most jealous.
>   If it be so, and many living sweare it,
>   It takes no little from the actor's merit,
>   Since, as the Moore is jealous of his wife,
>   Field can display the passion to the life."

He died on February 20th, 1633, at the age of
forty-six.

Neither his artistic career nor his life was of long
duration, but it seems as if they must have been full of
excitement, fame and variety.   His portrait shows us a
narrow, nervous and refined head, beautiful and expressive, a genuine " decadence " head, compared with
the quiet firmness of Burbage and Shakespeare.

Was not Field the very type of the highly gifted

---

[1] Reproduced from a MS. by J. P. Collier.   Its genuineness, as far as I
know, has not been disputed.

16—Nathaniel Field.

decadent, in whom the great art of the time blazed forth
with a brief but glorious light?

At all events, with Field and his generation, men
like Swanston, Benfield and Pollart, we come to the end
of the most important period of the history of the English
theatre.

At the same moment a period was drawing to a close
in politics, the long struggle between King and Parliament; and as the winning side was not favourably
inclined towards the theatres, it wrote an emphatic "Finis"
under the history both of the monarchy and of the stage.

On the 2nd of September 1642 Parliament issued the
following order :—

"Whereas the distressed Estate of Ireland, steeped
in her own Blood, and the distracted Estate of England,
threatened with a cloud of Blood, by a Civill Warre, call
for all possible meanes to appease and avert the Wrath
of God appearing in these Judgments; amongst which
Fasting and Prayer have been often tried to be very
effectual, have been lately, and are still enjoyned, and
whereas publike Sports doe not well agree with publike
Calamities, nor publike Stage-playes with the Seasons
of Humiliation, this being an Exercise of sad and pious
solemnity, and the other being Spectacles of, too commonly expressing lacivious Mirth and Levitie. It is
therefore thought fit, and Ordeined by the Lords and
Commons in this Parliament Assembled, that while these
sad Causes and set times of Humiliation doe continue,
publike Stage-playes shall cease, and bee forborne.
Instead of which are recommended to the people of this
Land, the profitable and seasonable Considerations of

Repentance, Reconciliation, and peace with God, which probably may produce outward peace and prosperity, and bring again Times of Joy and Gladness to these Nations." [1]

This was the death-blow of the theatres and dramatic art of the Shakespearean period.

Resistance was indeed attempted for a time, in the hope that this decree would be no more enforced than so many of its predecessors. But it soon became evident that the times had changed. A number of successive orders, each severer than the last, was directed against the unfortunate actors. First, they are threatened with imprisonment; then all actors are declared to be *ipso facto* "rogues and vagabonds"; if any man is found acting, he is to be punished with a flogging, and every person who is present at a play has to pay a fine of five shillings; the magistrates are authorised to pull down galleries and seats; in short, dramatic art is to be deprived of every support; and the actors, who were naturally nearly all of them staunch royalists, were persecuted like noxious animals.

Some of them became soldiers and fought in the war on the royalist side; others went to the Continent, and endeavoured to gain a living there.

From 1647 we may say that dramatic art was definitely suppressed in England, till it awoke to new life under the Restoration.

---

[1] This document is very rare. I believe it has not been reprinted anywhere but in Joseph Knight's edition of *Roscius Anglicanus*, from which we reproduce it here. Knight took his reproduction from a copy possessed by the booksellers, Jarvis & Son.

BIBLIOGRAPHY

The Alleyn Papers. A collection of original documents illustrative of the life and time of Edward Alleyn, and of the early English stage and drama. With an introduction by J. Paine Collier. London 1843

Archer, William: A Sixteenth Century Playhouse (*The Universal Review*). London 1888.

Barton Baker, H.: The London Stage. Its History and Traditions. 2 vols. London 1889.

Boas, F. S.: Shakespeare and his Predecessors. London 1895.

Bolte, Johannes: Englische Komödianten in Dänemark und Schweden.— Shakesp. Jahrb. Bd. XXIII.

„   Englische Komödianten in Münster und Ulm, ibid. Bd. XXXVI.

Brandes, Georg: William Shakespeare. 3 vols. København 1895. 1 vol. London 1899.

Cohn, Albert: Shakespeare in Germany in the Sixteenth and Seventeenth Centuries. London 1865.

„   Englische Komödianten in Köln (1562-1656). — Shakesp. Jahrb. Bd. XXI.

Collier, J. P.: Memoirs of Edward Alleyn, Founder of Dulwich College. London 1841.

„   Fools and Jesters, with a reprint of Robert Arnim's Nest of Ninnies 1608. London 1842.

„   The History of English Dramatic Poetry to the Time of Shakespeare and Annals of the Stage to the Restoration. 3 vols. London 1879.

Conrad, Hermann: Robert Greene als Dramatiker.—Shakesp. Jahrb. Bd. XIXX-XXX.

Creizenach, W.: Geschichte des neueren Dramas (Mittelalter und Frühre-naissance). Halle 1899.

Cunningham, Peter: Extracts from the Accounts of the Revels at Court in the Reign of Queen Elizabeth and King James I. London 1842.

Dewischeit, Curt: Shakespeare und die Stenographie (" Münchener Allg. Zeitung" 1898, No. 31).

Dyce, Alexander: Kemp's Nine Daies Wonder, performed in a Daunce from London to Norwich. With an Introduction and Notes.

„   Shakespeare's Works. With an Introduction and Notes 9 vols. London 1857.

Elze, Karl: Eine Aufführung in Globus Theater.—Shakesp. Jahrb. Bd. XIV.

Fleay, Frederick Gard: Shakespeare Manual. London 1878.
„ A Biographical Chronicle of the English Drama 1559-1642. 2 vols. London 1891.

Fuller, Thomas: The History of the Worthies of England. London MDCLXII.

Gaedertz, Th.: Zur Kenntniss der altenglischen Bühne, etc. Bremen 1888.

Genée, Rudolph: Shakespeares Liv og Værker. København 1877.

Gosson, Stephen: The School of Abuse, containing a Pleasant Invective against Poets, Pipers, Players, Jesters, etc. London 1841 (Shakespeare Society Reprint).

Greenstreet, James: The Blackfriars Playhouse: Its Antecedents (*Athenæum* No. 3141).
„ Blackfriars Theatre in the time of Shakespeare (*Athenæum* No. 3154 and 3156).

Guizot, Fr.-P.: Histoire de la Révolution d'Angleterre. Paris 1826.
„ Shakespeare et son temps. Paris 1852.

Halliwell, I. O.: Tarlton's Jest and News out of Purgatory. London 1844.
„ Outlines of the Life of Shakespeare, 3rd edit. London 1883.

Hansen, Adolf: En Notits om engelske Instrumentister ved Frederik den andens Hof. "Tilskueren" Juli 1900.

Harrison: Description of England in Shakespeare's Youth. Edited by Fr. J. Furnivall. London 1877.

Heywood, Thomas: An Apology for Actors. In three books. London 1841 (Shakespeare Society Reprint).

The Diary of *Philip Henslowe*, from 1591 to 1609. Edited by J. P. Collier. London 1845.

Jonson, Ben: Works. Edited by W. Gifford. 9 vols. London 1816.

Jullien, Adolphe: Les Spectateurs sur le théâtre. Paris 1875.

Jusserand, J.-J.: Le théâtre en Angleterre depuis la Conquête jusqu'aux prédécesseurs immédiats de Shakespeare. Paris 1881.

Kalisch, C.: Shakespeares yngre Samtidige og Efterfølgere. København 1890.

Kellner, L.: Shakespeare. Leipzig, Berlin, Wien 1900.

Klein, J. L.: Geschichte des englischen Dramas. Leipzig 1876.

Kurz, Hermann: Shakespeare der Schauspieler.—Shakesp. Jahrb. Bd. VI.

Laing, David: Notes on Ben Jonson's Conversations with William Drummond. London 1842.

Lee, Sidney: A Life of William Shakespeare. Illustrated Library Edition. London 1899.

Loftie, W. J.: A History of London. 2 vols. London 1884.

Malone, Edmund: Historical Account of the rise and progress of the English Stage. 3 vols. 1800.

Marston, John: Works. Edited by A. H. Bullen. 3 vols. London 1887.

Meissner, Johannes: Die englischen Komödianten in Oesterreich.—Shakesp. Jahrb. Bd. XIX.

Moulton, Rich. G.: Shakespeare as a Dramatic Artist. London 1885.

Møller, Niels: Shakespeares Theater ("Frem" Maj 1900).

Nash, Thomas: Pierce Penniless's Supplication to the Devil. Edit. by J. P. Collier. London 1842.

Northbrooke's Treatise against Dicing, Dancing, Plaies and Interludes, etc. Edit. by J. P. Collier. London 1843.

Ordish, T. Fairman: Early London Theatres (in the Fields). London 1894.

„　　Shakespeare's London. A Study of London in the Reign of Queen Elizabeth. London 1897.

Pepys, Samuel: Diary and Correspondence. Edited by Richard Lord Braybrooke. In five volumes. London 1851.

Prynne, William: Histriomastix. The Players Scourge; or, Actors Tragædie divided into Two Parts. London 1633.

Prölss, R.: Geschichte des neueren Dramas. Leipzig 1881-1883.

Ravn, V. C.: "Engelske Instrumentister" ved det danske Hof paa Shakespeares Tid. ("For Idé og Virkelighed" 1870 I.).

Sarrazin, G.: Zur Chronologie von Shakespeares Jugenddramen.—Shakesp. Jahrb. XXIX-XXX.

Schück, Henrik: William Shakespeare, hans lif och verksamhet. Stockholm 1883.

Stowe, John: Annales of England. London 1631.

Swinburne, A. C.: A Study of Ben Jonson. London 1889.

Thornbury, G. W.: Shakespere's England; or, Sketches of our Social History in the Reign of Elizabeth. London 1856.

Thümmel, Julius: Ueber Shakespeares Narren.—Shakesp. Jahrb. Bd. IX.

„　　Ueber Shakespeares Clowns.—Ibid. Bd. XI.

Vatke, Th.: Das Theater und das Londoner Publikum in Shakespeares Zeit.—Shakesp. Jahrb. Bd. XXI.

Ward, A. W.: A History of English dramatic literature to the death of Queen Anne. London 1875.

INDEX